THE PYTHON BIBLE FOR BEGINNERS

A Step-By-Step Guide to Master Coding from Scratch in Less Than 7 Days and Become the Expert that Top Companies Vie to Hire

(with Hands-On Exercises and Code Snippets)

TABLE OF CONTENTS

Chapter 1 - How to install, set up and run Python

Introduction to Python

Basically, there are three main types of programming languages: higher-level programming languages, lower-level programming languages, and assembly languages. Assembly languages are very easy for any computer to understand, while higher-level programming languages are easy for humans because their syntax is similar to simple English sentences.

Python is an object-oriented and high-level programming language, which means it is easy for us to learn and understand. Object-oriented programming, also called "OOP", is a programming language model based on objects rather than functions and logic. For now, you don't need to be confused about OOP; we will cover it in detail in upcoming tutorials.

Python is widely used in every field and development process, including server-side web development, mathematical calculations, scripting, software development, and game development. Nowadays, Python is popular for its widespread use in data science and machine learning.

Why is Python a popular programming language?

Despite having many applications and modules, Python is an open-source community language, and anyone can download and use it. Before installing and setting up Python on our system, let's see the key features that make Python one of the most famous programming languages:

- You can use it is several fields and for tons of different tasks, including web applications, game development, machine learning, software development, and more.
- It assists with complex mathematics and big data processing.
- Another essential feature of Python is its compatibility with a variety of platforms (for example Mac, Windows, Linux, Raspberry Pi, and many others).
- It is a high-level language, and its syntax closely resembles English, making it easy for beginners.
- It offers a plethora of built-in modules, eliminating the need to code everything from scratch.

How to install Python on Windows

Installing Python on Windows is straightforward. Begin by selecting the desired version of Python from the official Python site (www.python.org) in the download section. It's advisable to choose the latest version for the most recent updates. After installation, verify the Python version using the commands below in the IDE:

```python
from platform import python_version

print("Version of Python is:", python_version())
```

output:

Version of Python is: 3.10.6

As seen here, the version of Python is 3.10.6 in our case. For the moment, you don't need to understand this code in depth; we will discuss its specifics in an upcoming tutorial; it is just one of the ways you can follow in order to get Python installed on your computer.

How to install Python on Linux

In this case, the good news is that Python comes pre-installed. To check the Python version on Linux, write the following commands in your terminal.

```
python3 -V
```

Output:

In our case, the version is 3.10.6. If Python is not installed on your system, you can run the following commands in the terminal to install Python.

```
sudo apt-get install python3
```

In case you need a specific version of Python, you can simply specify it in the code:

```
sudo apt-get install python3.8
#or
sudo apt-get install python3.9
```

Installing Jupyter notebook

To write, compile, and run Python code, we need a text editor. When you install Python on Windows, it comes with a default IDE where you can write and run your code. However, this default IDE is not interactive.

There are various useful IDEs that can make coding easier. We will be using Jupyter Notebook, a software that allows users to compile all components of a data project in one place. This makes it much easier to demonstrate the entire process of a project to your intended audience. Additionally, users can generate data visualizations and other components to share with others via this web-based application.

If you wish to install Jupyter Notebook on Windows, it is recommended to first install the Anaconda distribution:

- Go to the official Anaconda website and download the distribution for your system by following the instructions provided (https://www.anaconda.com/products/distribution).

- Once the download is complete, congratulations, Jupyter Notebook is also installed.

You can either open Anaconda and run Jupyter Notebook from there or open the command line and run the following commands to launch Jupyter Notebook:

Once launched, the Jupyter Notebook interface will appear in your web browser; this is what Jupyter Notebook looks like.

Now, let us step by step understand how to create a notebook and run Python code in it

Run your first Python file

Once Jupyter Notebook is open, click on the "new" button at the top right side to generate a new Python file. This is what a new file in Jupyter Notebook looks like:

In a similar way, you can choose to work with any text editor or IDE for Python; the steps will be the same. Open the IDE, create a new file with a .py extension, and open the file to start writing Python code.

Now, let's write our first program in Python in Jupyter Notebook and run it:

```
print('Hello world!')
```

You can run the code either by clicking the run button in the toolbar or by pressing Shift+Enter on your keyboard. The program above will print 'Hello world!'.

```
In [4]: print('Hello world!')
        Hello world!
```

Chapter 2 - First Steps Toward Learning Python Language

Now, let's start with Python by writing 'Hello my friends'. Open your Jupyter Notebook, generate a new notebook or open the previous one, and write this line in order to print 'Hello my friends':

```
print('Hello my friends')
```

Output:

```
Hello my friends
```

The **print()** function in Python takes any argument and prints it to the user. We will cover functions in detail in upcoming tutorials. Try printing information about yourself, including your name and age, using Python, as shown below:

```
print("Hi! This is Peter and I am 22. I am majoring in computer science")
```

Output:

```
Hi! This is Peter and I am 22. I am majoring in computer science
```

As you can see, we printed the desired information in one single line. However, we can also print the information over multiple lines. In Python, **\n** is used to move to the next line. Now, let's try to print the same information over several different lines.

```
print("Hi! This is Peter. \nI am 22. \nI am majoring in computer science")
```

Output:

```
Hi! This is Peter.
I am 22.
I am majoring in computer science
```

We successfully printed information over multiple lines using '\n'.

Statement in Python

In Python, anything that we write is a statement; in other words, it is a precise instruction that the Python interpreter will execute. So far, we have learned only one statement: **print()**. Python executes statements line by line. If there are multiple lines of statements, then Python will execute the statements line by line to produce the results.

Consider this code, where we'll use multiple print statements:

```
print('hello')
print('I am Peter')
print('Hope everything is fine!')
```

Output:

```
hello
I am Peter
Hope everything is fine!
```

As you can see, we have got multiple lines of output.

Comments

Comments in Python are statements that are completely ignored by the interpreter and are usually added to explain a certain piece of code. Single-line comments in Python start with a hashtag #, meaning any statement that starts with # will be considered a comment and ignored by the interpreter.

For example, if we consider the following simple program, comments are used to explain the code:

```
# greeting with people
print('Hello!')
print('Hope you are doing great!')
```

Running this program will produce the following output:

```
Hello!
```

```
Hope you are doing great!
```

As you can see, the first line has been ignored by the interpreter because it is a comment.

To add multiple lines of comments, you can either use the hashtag at the beginning of each line or use triple quotation marks. Here's an example using hashtags:

```
# this is multiple line comments
# greeting with people
# the code asks how are you
print('How are you?')
```

The Python interpreter will only execute the print statement.

And here's how you can use triple quotation marks for multiple lines of comments:

```
''' this is a multiple lines comment
greeting with people
the code asks how are you'''


print('How are you?')
```

Anything written inside triple quotation marks will be considered as comments in Python.

User-input

Up to now, we have learned how to print information to the user. Now we'll see how to take input from the user and display their message using the input() method. Here's an example asking the user for their name:

```
input('Enter your name Please: ')
```

When we run the above code, we get a message prompting the user to enter their name:

```
Enter your name Please: [                          ]
```

This program will display a message and provide a space for the user to input their name. Anything written inside the **input()** method will be displayed to the user. In this case, the message is 'Enter your name, please'.

It's important to store input values from the user in computer memory so we can use them later. In Python, we store information in variables. We will cover variables in more detail in the next section; for now, just understand that variables are used for storing information.

Here's how you can take input from the user, store it in a variable, and print the message:

```
name = input('Enter your name Please: ')


print('Your name is :', name)
```

Output:

```
Your name is : Peter
```

In the first line, we are asking the user to enter their name and storing their input in a variable. Finally, we use the **print()** method to display the information back to the user.

Printing basic information exercise

Now that we have learned how to print information, take user input, and then save it in a variable, we can build a small form to gather and display basic information about a student. We will also explain each step using Python comments.

```
# taking user name and storing it in a variable
name = input("What is your name? ")


# taking age from user
age = input('What is your age? ')
```

```
# asking for favorite color and season
color = input('What is your favorite color? ')
season = input('What is your favorite season? ')
```

Output:

```
What is your name? Peter
What is your age? 22
What is your favorite color? Red
What is your favorite season? spring
```

This is the information that we have gathered from the user. Now, let us display this information using a print statement:

```
print('--------Student info center-------------')
print('Name :', name)
print('age  :', age)
print('Favorite color : ', color)
print('Favorite season: ', season)
```

Output:

```
--------Student info center-------------
Name : Peter
age  : 22
Favorite color :  Red
Favorite season:  spring
```

As you can see, we have successfully gathered and displayed the information provided by the user.

Chapter 3 - Python Variables and Basic arithmetic operations

What is a Python variable?

To understand the concept of a Python variable, imagine this scenario: You're preparing for school by gathering your pen, notebooks, books, etc., and placing everything in your bag to carry with you. Anytime you need something, you reach into your bag and take it out. Similarly, a variable in Python is something where you can save information inside, and when you need to use that specific information in your program, you can simply refer to the corresponding variable.

Formally, a variable in Python is a symbolic name acting as a reference or pointer to an object. Assigning a variable to an object is akin to naming the object, allowing you to refer to it by the given name from that point onward. Don't be daunted by the terms "pointer" and "object"; we will delve into them in upcoming sections. For now, just understand that a variable is a named reference to a specific piece of stored information.

Different Data types of variables in Python

In this section, we will cover three basic data types of variables: integers, floats, and strings.

- **Integers**: In Python, an integer is a whole number without any decimal points, which can be positive, negative, or zero. For example:

```
# Examples of integers in variables
num1 =10
num2 = 23
num3 = -198
num4 = 0
```

Python doesn't require you to specify a variable's data type when declaring it. You simply give the variable a name and assign data to it.

- **Floats:** Floats represent floating-point numbers, which are numbers with a decimal point. For instance:

```
# Examples of floating points
float1 = 4.32
float2 = -324.6
foat3 = 4564.0
```

As you can see, these variables successfully store floating-point numbers.

- **Strings**: In Python 3, anything enclosed in double or single quotation marks will be read as a string. For example:

```
# Examples of string data type
str1 = 'This is bashir'
str2 ='B'
str3 ="10"
str4 ='4.32'
```

Notice that even when numbers are assigned to variables with quotation marks, they are treated as strings, not floats or integers.

Input different data types from user

In a previous tutorial, we learned how to take input from the user. However, we didn't discuss how to receive different types of data. Now, we'll cover how to input floats and integers.

- **String**: Taking a string input is straightforward. Simply use the **input** method:

```
str1 = input('Please enter your name: ')
```

The entered information is automatically considered a string.

- **Integer**: To receive an integer, explicitly convert the input using the **int()** function:

```
int1 = int(input('Please enter your age: '))
```

Output:

```
Please enter your age: 34
```

The **int()** function converts the input to an integer type. If the user provides a non-integer input, the program will return an error due to a type mismatch.

```
Please enter your age: Bashir

- - - - - - - - - - - - - - - - - - - - - - - - - - - - - - - - - - - - - - - - - - -
ValueError                              Traceback (most recent call last)
/tmp/ipykernel_21210/2567655306.py in <module>
----> 1 int1 = int(input('Please enter your age: '))

ValueError: invalid literal for int() with base 10: 'Bashir'
```

Similarly, when we need to receive a floating-point number from the user, we must explicitly specify the expected data type by utilizing the **float()** method.

```
float1 = float(input("Enter any decimal number: "))
```
Output:

```
Enter any decimal number: 3.32
```
As you can see, we entered a floating point.

Basic arithmetic operations

Performing basic arithmetic operations in Python is quite easy. We just have to use the symbol of the operation between multiple values. For example, let us add two numeric values together.

```
print(4+5)
```
This will print 9. All the other basic arithmetic operations work in a similar way.

Addition and Subtraction

Now, we will create different variables and use those variables to perform addition and subtraction operations.

```
var1 = 30
var2 = 5
var3 = 5.5

print(var1+var2)
print(var3-var2)
```

Output:

```
35
0.5
```

As you can see, in the first print statement, we have added two integers, while in the second print statement, we subtracted an integer value from a floating-point value, resulting in another floating-point value.

If we add two string data types, the result will be the combination of both values, as shown below:

```
str1 = 'This is '
str2 = 'Bashir'

print(str1 + str2)
```

Output:

```
This is Bashir
```

However, a problem arises when we try to add different data types with a string value. See the example below:

```
str1 = 'my age is '
int1 = 22

print(str1 + int1)
```

Output:

```
- - - - - - - - - - - - - - - - - - - - - - - - - - - - - - - - - - - - - - - - - - - - - - -
TypeError                              Traceback (most recent call last)
/tmp/ipykernel_72719/3276559825.py in <module>
      2 int1 = 22
      3
----> 4 print(str1 + int1)

TypeError: can only concatenate str (not "int") to str
```

In this case, we get an error because an integer value cannot be added to a string value. So, in some cases while performing addition and subtraction, make sure that the values have the same data type.

We can add a numeric value to a string by converting its data type to a string, as shown below:

```
str1 = 'my age is '
int1 = 22


print(str1 + str(int1))
```

Output:

```
my age is 22
```

This time, we were able to add a numeric value to the string by converting its type to a string.

Multiplication and division

Let's now apply multiplication to two numeric values in Python.

```
var1 = 5
var2 = 10


print(var1*var2)
```

Output:

```
50
```

The division of two numbers in Python is also simple. See the example below:

```
var1 = 5
var2 = 10
var3 = 3

print(var2/var1)
print(var2/var3)
```

Output:

```
2.0
3.3333333333333335
```

As you can see, we get the answer as a floating-point.

Chapter 4 - Python Data Types

In Python, data types help us categorize and classify data based on what kind of value they hold. This categorization also indicates what operations are possible with that data. For example, you can add two numbers but not necessarily two pieces of text: with numerical data, you can execute mathematical operations such as addition or subtraction, while with textual data (strings), you might concatenate (join them together) or capitalize them.

As said in the introduction, Python is considered an object-oriented programming language, which means everything in Python is treated as an object. This is a fundamental concept, making it easier to organize and manage code. In object-oriented programming, a 'class' can be thought of as a blueprint or prototype. For example, if you have a class called 'Dog', it might represent general characteristics and behaviors that all dogs have. An 'instance' or 'object' is a specific realization of that class. So, if 'Buddy' and 'Bella' are objects of the 'Dog' class, we know that they both are dogs, but each has specific attributes like color, breed, etc. In Python, when you have a variable that holds a number, the number's data type (like integer or float) is actually a class, and the variable itself is an instance or object of that class.

In other words, when we talk about data types in Python, we're referring to classes; when we create a variable, it becomes an instance or an object of that class. This means the variable inherits the properties and behaviors of the class it belongs to.

We have the following data types:

- Text Type:
  - Str
- Numeric data type
  - Integer
  - Float
  - Complex
- Sequence data types

- o List
- o Tuple
- Mapping
  - o Dictionary
- Set Types
  - o Set
  - o Frozenset
- Boolean types
  - o True
  - o False

Python numeric data types

We have already discussed some of the numeric data types in the previous chapter. The third numeric data type that we still have to analyze is the complex number, which is represented by "x + yi". In Python, the **complex()** method converts real numbers into complex numbers. Consider the following example to learn how to build complex numbers in Python.

```
real = 34
imaginary = 4


complex_number = complex(real, imaginary)


print(complex_number)
```

Output:

```
(34+4j)
```

As you can see, the output consists of both real and imaginary parts.

Let's explore now the built-in method called **type()** that returns the data type of a variable.

Let's create two variables with different data types and use the **type()** method to determine their respective data types

```
var1 = 10
var2 = 3.3


print('Data type of var1 is : ', type(var1))
print('Data type of var2 is : ', type(var2))
```

Output:

```
Data type of var1 is :  <class 'int'>
Data type of var2 is :  <class 'float'>
```

As you can see, the first variable is of integer data type, while the second is of floating-point data type because it contains decimal points.

If we want to check the complex data type using the **type()** function:

```
print(type(complex_number))
```

Output:

```
<class 'complex'>
```

Python list data type

In Python, a list serves as a versatile container for holding a variety of items under a single variable, accommodating also values of diverse data types.

We use square brackets to declare lists as shown below:

```
list1 =[]
```

Now, we can add items inside the square brackets, and they will be stored in list1.

```
list1 =[1, 2, 3, 4, 5, 6 ,7 ,8, 9 ,10]


print(list1)
```

Output:

```
[1, 2, 3, 4, 5, 6, 7, 8, 9, 10]
```

Each item in the list should be separated by commas.

As we discussed earlier, a list can contain items of different data types. Let's create a list that includes integers, floats, and string values.

```
list2 = [1, 2, 3, 'a', 'b', 'c', 2.2, 3.3, 4.4]


print(list2)
```

Output:

```
[1, 2, 3, 'a', 'b', 'c', 2.2, 3.3, 4.4]
```

Another way to add items to the list is using **append()** method. This method adds different items to the list one by one as shown below:

```
list3 =[]


a =2
b =3
c ='A'


list3.append(a)
list3.append(b)
list3.append(c)
```

```
print(list3)
```

Output:

```
[2, 3, 'A']
```

We initially created an empty list and then defined various variables. We used the append method to add these variables to the empty list.

We can also use a "for" loop to append items to the list if we want to create a list within a specific range.

Please note: The structure of the "for" loop will be discussed in more detail in Chapter 7.

```
list4 =[]

for i in range(10):
    list4.append(i)

print(list4)
```

Output:

```
[0, 1, 2, 3, 4, 5, 6, 7, 8, 9]
```

We created an empty list and then employed the for loop to append items from that specific range.

Another important feature of lists is nested lists. A nested list is essentially a list within another list. Let's see an example:

```
list5 = [[1,2,3,4], ['', 'b', 'c'], [2.2, 3.3, 4.4]]
```

```
print(list5)
```

Output:

```
[[1, 2, 3, 4], ['', 'b', 'c'], [2.2, 3.3, 4.4]]
```

With the for loop we can create nested list as well:

```
list6=[]

for i in range (1, 5):
    list7 = []
    for j in range(i):
        list7.append(j)
    list6.append(list7)


print(list6)
```

Output:

```
[[0], [0, 1], [0, 1, 2], [0, 1, 2, 3]]
```

Python tuple data

Tuples in Python, like lists, store multiple items within a single variable. However, tuples are immutable ordered collections, meaning their elements cannot be changed once set. Python represents tuples using round brackets, as shown in this example:

```
tup1 =()

print(type(tup1))
```

Output:

```
<class 'tuple'>
```

Let's add items to the tuple and print it:

28

```
tup1 = (1, 2, 3, 4, 5, 6, 7)


print(tup1)
```

Output:

```
(1, 2, 3, 4, 5, 6, 7)
```

Unlike lists, you cannot use the append() method to add new elements to a tuple. Instead, you can utilize the '+' operator to concatenate elements.

```
tup1 = ()


tup1 = tup1 + (1,)
tup1= tup1 +(2,)
tup1 =tup1 + (3,)


print(tup1)
```

Output:

```
(1, 2, 3)
```

Now, let's create a nested tuple using a for loop. A nested tuple contains another tuple within it.
Please note: The structure of the "for" loop will be discussed in more detail in Chapter 5.5.

```
tup2 = ()

for i in range(1, 5):
    tup3 = ()
    for j in range(i):
        tup3 = tup3 + (j,)
    tup2 = tup2 + (tup3,)
```

```
print(tup2)
```

Output:

```
((0,), (0, 1), (0, 1, 2), (0, 1, 2, 3))
```

Python Dictionary data type

A dictionary in Python is a collection of key-value pairs, functioning similarly to a map. Unlike some data types that store just a single value per element, a dictionary can hold multiple values associated with distinct keys.

Curly brackets denote a dictionary, as shown below:

```
dict1 = {}

print(type(dict1))
```

Output:

```
<class 'dict'>
```

In dictionaries, items are paired as key-value: the key comes first, followed by a colon, then the associated value. A simple dictionary example is provided below:

```
dict1 = {'A' :1, "B" : 2, "C":3}

print(dict1)
```

Output:

```
{'A': 1, 'B': 2, 'C': 3}
```

It's essential that keys in a dictionary remain unique; if duplicate keys are present, the last instance of that key is retained.

30

```
dict1 = {'A': 1, "B": 2, "A": 3}


print(dict1)
```

Output:

```
{'A': 3, 'B': 2}
```

As you can see, there were two keys with the same name, but at the end we obtained only the last one.

Notably, dictionary values can be of varying data types, such as lists, tuples, or even other dictionaries.

```
dict1 = {'A' :(1,2, 3, 4, 5), "B" : [1,2,3,4,5]}


print(dict1)
```

Output:

```
{'A': (1, 2, 3, 4, 5), 'B': [1, 2, 3, 4, 5]}
```

For instance, the values in the provided dictionary are a tuple and a list, respectively.

A nested dictionary contains another dictionary within it:

```
dict1 = {'A' :{'a':1, 'b':2}, "B" : {'c':3, 'd':4}}


print(dict1)
```

Output:

```
{'A': {'a': 1, 'b': 2}, 'B': {'c': 3, 'd': 4}}
```

As you can see, dict1 has two separate dictionaries inside it.

Two helpful methods associated with dictionaries are **keys()** and **values()**. The keys() method retrieves all the dictionary's keys as a list:

```
dict1 = {'A' :{'a':1, 'b':2}, "B" : {'c':3, 'd':4}}


print(dict1.keys())
```

Output:

```
dict_keys(['A', 'B'])
```

The values() method yields a list of all the dictionary's values.

```
dict1 = {'A' :{'a':1, 'b':2}, "B" : {'c':3, 'd':4}}


print(dict1.values())
```

Output:

```
dict_values([{'a': 1, 'b': 2}, {'c': 3, 'd': 4}])
```

Python Boolean type

Python's Boolean type is a built-in data type that can take on one of two values (True or False) and represents the truth value of an expression, such as whether 6>4 (this will return False) or 4<7 (this will return True). Typically, Booleans are employed in conditional statements.

```
a = False
b = True
print(type(a))
print(type(b))
```

Output:

```
<class 'bool'>
<class 'bool'>
```

Booleans are useful when comparing things. See the example below:

```
a = 10
b =19
print(a==b)
```

Output:

```
False
```

Of course, we get false because 10 is not equal to 19.

Python Sets

In mathematics, sets are organized collections of objects and can be represented in either set-builder form or roster form. In Python, sets are similar to lists, but they contain only unique elements. Python has a built-in method to create sets: **set()**

```
set1 = set()
print(type(set1))
```

Output:

```
<class 'set'>
```

Let's create a simple set and print its elements:

```
set1 = set([5,6,7,8,9,10,11])
print(set1)
```

Output:

```
{5, 6, 7, 8, 9, 10, 11}
```

As mentioned earlier, sets hold only unique items and if we add duplicate elements to a set, they will be removed.

```
set1 = set([5,5,5,5,6,6,6,6,6,6,7,8,9,10,11])
print(set1)
```

Output:

{5, 6, 7, 8, 9, 10, 11}

As you can observe, the duplicate elements are no longer present.

Chapter 5 - Basic operations

In this section, we will delve into various operations related to Python data types that we introduced in the previous chapter. More specifically, we'll explore how indexing works, how to retrieve specific elements from lists or dictionaries, and how to add and remove elements.

Operations on a list
You're already acquainted with lists, which can store multiple items in a single variable. Let's begin by creating two lists and then adding them together.

```
List_1a = [9,10,11,12]
List_2a = [12,13,14,15]


List_3a = list_1a + list2_2a


print(list_3a)
```
Output:
```
[9, 10, 11, 12, 12, 13, 14, 15]
```

As you can observe, the addition operator combines the elements from each list and produces a new list containing all the items. This approach offers a straightforward way to merge lists. However, if we attempt direct subtraction or multiplication between two lists, it results in an error; in fact, Python doesn't support multiplication on sequence types.

Indexing of list
In Python, indexing starts at zero. Every item in a list is systematically placed in sequence, commencing with zero. For instance, suppose we have a specific list, and our goal is to access its first element. This can be achieved by pinpointing its position via indexing. The first item of the list is represented by an index value of 0, while the second by an index of 1, and so forth.

```
list1 = ['A', 'B', 'C', 'D', 'E', 'F']

first_element = list1[0]

print(first_element)
```

Output:

```
A
```

As you can see, accessing the first element requires referencing its index value.

Negative indexing is also supported. In this system, -1 represents the last element, -2 stands for the second-to-last element, and so on.

```
list1 = ['A', 'B', 'C', 'D', 'E', 'F']

last_element = list1[-1]

print(first_element)
```

Output:

```
F
```

We accessed the list's last item using negative indexing. You can try to access different elements from the list using different indexing values.

Let's take it a step further and extract items from nested lists through indexing. If we create a nested list and fetch the item at index 0, we retrieve the entire inner list. This inner list is perceived as the primary list's first element.

```
list1 = [['A', 'B', 'C'], ['D', 'E', 'F'] ,['G', "H"]]

first_element = list1[0]

print(first_element)
```

Output:

```
['A', 'B', 'C']
```

To extract the 'A' element, double indexing is necessary, which entails first accessing the inner list and then the specific element within it.

```
list1 = [['A', 'B', 'C'], ['D', 'E', 'F'] ,['G', "H"]]


first_element = list1[0][0]


print(first_element)
```

Output:

```
A
```

Similarly, to access the 'F' element, we first reference the nested list, followed by the specific item within, as demonstrated below.

```
list1 = [['A', 'B', 'C'], ['D', 'E', 'F'] ,['G', "H"]]


first_element = list1[1][-1]


print(first_element)
```

Output:

```
F
```

Play around with diverse indexing approaches to understand the mechanics better.

Slicing the list using indexing

Slicing in Python is a potent tool for extracting sequence segments, be it strings, tuples, or lists. Here, we'll focus on list slicing. To illustrate, imagine a list where we desire a sub-list comprising its initial three items.

36

```
list1 = [1,2,3,4,5,6,7,8,9]


#slicing the list
sliced = list1[0:3]


print(sliced)
```

Output:

```
[1, 2, 3]
```

Through slicing, we extract a sub-list embodying the primary list's first three elements. Inside the square brackets, specifying list1[0:3] means the sub-list should span from index 0 to 3.

To retrieve the last 4 list items, the [-4:] notation suffices: this will return the list's final 4 elements.

```
list1 = [1,2,3,4,5,6,7,8,9]


#slicing the list
sliced = list1[-4:]
 print(sliced)
```

Output:

```
[6, 7, 8, 9]
```

Let's see how to apply slicing to a nested list. Suppose we have a nested list and we want to extract the last 2 elements.

```
list1 = [[1,2],[3,4],[5,6],[7,8,9]]


#slicing the list
sliced = list1[-2:]

```

```
print(sliced)
```

Output:

```
[[5, 6], [7, 8, 9]]
```

The result contains the two final nested lists.

If our goal is to pinpoint the final 2 elements of the last nested list, we have to use a precise specification:

```
list1 = [[1,2],[3,4],[5,6],[7,8,9]]

#slicing the list
sliced = list1[-2:][1][-2:]

print(sliced)
```

Output:

```
[8, 9]
```

Appending and deleting elements from list
Now we will learn how to add other elements to our list and delete the existing ones.

Among the several methods, we can mention the **append()** method, which is the most common one when the goal is to add elements to the list:

```
# empty list
list1 =[]

# adding elements
list1.append(10)
list1.append(20)
list1.append(30)
list1.append(40)
```

```
print(list1)
```

Output:

```
[10, 20, 30, 40]
```

Note that the append() method adds elements to the end. However, if you need to insert elements at a specific index, you can use the **insert()** method. This method requires two parameters: the first is used to indicate the required position, while the second represents the value of the element to be added.

```
list1 = [1,2,3,4,5,6,7,8,9]

# inserting new element
list1.insert(2, 'Peter')

print(list1)
```

Output:

```
[1, 2, 'Peter', 3, 4, 5, 6, 7, 8, 9]
```

Another handy method is **extend()**, very helpful when your goal is to add elements between 2 lists. For instance, let's consider two lists and suppose we want to create a third list that combines elements from both of them:

```
list1 = [1,2,3,4,5,6,7,8,9]
list2 = [10, 20, 30, 40]

# extend method
list1.extend(list2)
```

```
list1
```

Output:

```
[1, 2, 3, 4, 5, 6, 7, 8, 9, 10, 20, 30, 40]
```

Next, let's discuss how to remove elements from a list. One method for this is the **remove()** method, where you simply have to tell the system which is the element you intend to remove, as demonstrated below:

```
list1 = [1,2, 'Peter',3,4,5,6,7,8,9]

# removing elements
list1.remove('Peter')

print(list1)
```

Output:

```
[1, 2, 3, 4, 5, 6, 7, 8, 9]
```

Another way to remove items is the **pop()** method, which takes the index value of the element as a parameter. Consider that your goal is to remove the element at an index of 2. You would use this method:

```
list1 = [1,2, 'Peter',3,4,5,6,7,8,9]

# removing elements
list1.pop(2)

print(list1)
```

Output:

```
[1, 2, 3, 4, 5, 6, 7, 8, 9]
```

Moreover, we can also apply the "**del**" keyword to remove elements from a list, as shown below:

```
list1 = [1,2, 'Peter',3,4,5,6,7,8,9]


# deleting element
del list1[2]


print(list1)
```

Output:

```
[1, 2, 3, 4, 5, 6, 7, 8, 9]
```

Operation on string data type

String operations in Python have many parallels to those of lists. For example, you could concatenate 2 strings simply applying the addition operator, as shown below.

```
str1 ='John '
str2 = 'Alam'


str3 = str1+str2


print(str3)
```

Output:

```
John Alam
```

Indexing and slicing of string

Indexing and slicing in strings operate similarly to lists; let's create a string and use indexing to display its first and last characters:

```
str1 ='This is me'


first_element = str1[0]
```

```
last_element = str1[-1]


print('First element is :', first_element)
print('Last element is :', last_element)
```

Output:

```
First element is : T
Last element is : e
```

We can also extract substrings using slicing. For instance, let's retrieve the last name from a full name using this method."

```
str1 ='John Alam'


# slicing
last_name = str1[-4:]


print(last_name)
```

Output:

```
Alam
```

Note that we have used the negative indexing for slicing.

Operations on dictionaries

We know that in Python, dictionaries consist of key-value pairs. There are several useful methods available to perform a variety of operations on dictionaries. For instance, in order to remove a key-value pair from the dictionary, we can use the **del** keyword, as already seen before:

```
Dic = {'one': 1, "two":2, "three":3}


# deleting first element
del Dic['one']
```

```
print(Dic)
```

Output:

```
{'two': 2, 'three': 3}
```

The update() method modifies the original dictionary by integrating the key-value pairs from a second dictionary. If there are overlapping keys in both dictionaries, the values from the second dictionary take precedence, as shown below:

```
Dic1 = {'one': 1, "two":2, "three":3}
Dic2 = {'one': 10, "four":4, "five":5}


# updating the dic1
Dic1.update(Dic2)


print(Dic1)
```

Output:

```
{'one': 10, 'two': 2, 'three': 3, 'four': 4, 'five': 5}
```

Note how the value 10 has been associated with the first key because the second dictionary assigned this value to the identical key. The methods **keys()** and **values()** yield lists of the dictionary's keys and values, respectively. Let's use these methods to extract the lists of keys and values.

```
Dic1 = {'one': 1, "two":2, "three":3}


# getting keys
keys = Dic1.keys()


#getting values
values = Dic1.values()
```

```
print('Keys: ', keys)
print('Values: ', values)
```

Output:

```
Keys:  dict_keys(['one', 'two', 'three'])
Values:  dict_values([1, 2, 3])
```

Lastly, the **items()** method returns a list of tuples, where each tuple comprises a key and its corresponding value:

```
Dic1 = {'one': 1, "two":2, "three":3}


# getting items
items = Dic1.items()


print(items)
```

Output:

```
dict_items([('one', 1), ('two', 2), ('three', 3)])
```

Chapter 6 - Python classes

In programming language like python, a class is a code template used to create objects (a particular data structure); Objects have member variables (often referred to as attributes) and have behavior associated with them (usually implemented as functions or methods). In our past simple example, 'Buddy' and 'Bella' are objects of the 'Dog' class.

The **class** keyword is used to generate the class in Python. For example, let's build a very simple class which contains the variable x.

```
class variable:
   x = 10
```

Typically, the first docstring inside a class is used to describe the class's purpose (in fact you should always start a class with a docstring explaining its functionality):

```
class variable:
   '''This is a sample class which contains variable'''
   x = 10
```

Python attribute vs instance variable

We can identify 2 types of attributes in Python: class attributes and instance attributes.

Class attributes are variables that belong to the class itself, rather than to any specific object of that class; they are shared across all instances of the class and are defined outside the constructor method.

Instance attributes are variables that are specific to a single object of the class. These variables are only accessible within the scope of that particular object and are defined within the constructor function. For clarification, consider the Python class below with an instance variable:

```
# python class
class Student:


  # class attribute
  GPA = 3.54


  # constructor of class
  def __init__(self, name):


    # instance variable
    self.name = name
```

In the above example, the GPA is our class attribute while the name is our instance variable.

Attribute referencing in Python

Attribute referencing in Python classes follows the standard attribute reference syntax used elsewhere in Python: class_object.attribute_name.

In the following Python attribute referencing example, you'll see that we can access class attributes by prefixing them with the class name, followed by a dot.

```
# python class
class Student:


  # class attribute
  GPA = 3.54
  name = John Alam'


# referencing the attributes
print(Student.GPA)
print(Student.name)
```

Output:

```
3.54
John Alam
```

It's noteworthy that in this instance, we didn't create a new object; we merely accessed the attribute using the class name and dot notation.

Another approach to access class attributes is by creating objects of the class and then referencing the attributes via these objects. In the subsequent example, observe that we instantiate a new object and then access its attributes.

```python
# python class
class Student:

  # class attribute
  GPA = 3.54
  name = 'Bashir Alam'


# creating object
student1 = Student


# referencing the attributes
print(student1.GPA)
print(student1.name)
```

Output:

```
3.54
John Alam
```

Note that this time we created a new object and got access to the attributes using the object.

Constructors in Python

Within a class, to initialize an object when it's created, we can use the **constructor** method. In Python classes, some methods begin with double underscores. One such special method is __init__(); this function is automatically invoked whenever a new object of the class is instantiated and serves as the class's constructor. Let's create a Python class with a constructor:

```python
# Python class
class Student:

    # constuctor in python class
    def __init__(self, gpa, name):
        self.gpa = gpa
        self.name = name
```

Here there's an argument labeled "self." This argument always appears first, whether in a constructor or any other class method. It represents the instance of the class and consistently refers to the current object. Now, consider the following example to better understand how to use the 'self' keyword to access class attributes:

```python
# Python class
class Student:

    # constuctor in python class
    def __init__(self, gpa, name):
        self.gpa = gpa
        self.name = name

    # method
    def student_info(self):
        print('GPA : ', self.gpa)
```

```
    print('Name : ', self.name)


# creating objects
student1 = Student(3.4, 'Bashir')
student2 = Student(3.2, 'Alam')


student1.student_info()
student2.student_info()
```

Output:

GPA	:	3.4
Name	:	John
GPA	:	3.2
Name : Alam		

Modifying or deleting class attribute

After gaining access to attributes within a class, we can easily modify or delete them. In the following example we'll see how to alter an attribute inside a class.

```
# python class
class Student:


  # class attribute
  GPA = 3.54
  name = 'Bashir Alam'


# creating and object
student1 = Student


# printing before changing
print('GPA before changing: ', student1.GPA)
```

```
# changing the attribute
student1.GPA = 2.9


# printing after changing
print('GPA after changing: ', student1.GPA)
```

Output:

```
GPA before changing:  3.54
GPA after changing:  2.9
```

Note that we successfully changed the attribute's value by accessing it directly.

Additionally, we can remove the attribute using the del keyword, as demonstrated below:

```
# python class
class Student:

  # class attribute
  GPA = 3.54
  name = 'Bashir Alam'


# creating and object
student1 = Student


# printing before changing
print('GPA before changing: ', student1.GPA)


# deleting the attribute
del student1.GPA


# printing after changing
```

```
print('GPA after changing: ', student1.GPA)
```

Output:

```
GPA before changing:  3.54
--------------------------------------------------------------
AttributeError                       Traceback (most recent call last)
/tmp/ipykernel_302949/2871753056.py in <module>
     16
     17 # printing after changing
---> 18 print('GPA after changing: ', student1.GPA)

AttributeError: type object 'Student' has no attribute 'GPA'
```

Initially, we were able to display the attribute, but after employing the del keyword to remove it, subsequent attempts to access the attribute resulted in an error, indicating the attribute's absence

Chapter 7 - Loops in Python

Python's programming language offers 3 methods to execute loops for iterative solutions. While each method delivers similar basic functionality, their syntax and condition-checking times vary.

For loop / While loop / Nested loop

This section delves into Python loops, exploring their types, syntax, and functionality. Additionally, we'll practice coding using these loops.

Like in other programming languages, loops in Python are statements that execute a group of instructions repeatedly until a specified requirement/condition is met. Through loops, we can compress extensive code segments into just a few lines. For instance, to display "Welcome!" 50 times, we can utilize loops to set the repetition count rather than manually writing the print command 50 times.

The main difference is that for loop is input-controlled, while the while loop is output-controlled: Typically, for loops are employed when the iteration count is predetermined, whereas while loops are reserved for cases with indefinite iterations, terminating once a specific condition becomes true.

For loop

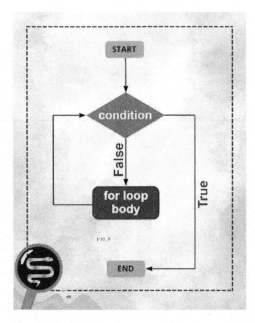

A for loop iterates over iterable objects, such as lists, tuples, dictionaries, sets, etc. It will execute loop operations for each element in the sequence, persisting until the sequence's end is reached. In Python, the for loop uses the 'in' keyword.

The syntax is presented below:

```
for item in iterator:

    statement(s)
```

Let's see how a **for** loop can be used to print "Welcome!" 10 times without redundantly invoking the print command on each occasion:

```
# creating a list of 10 items

list = [0, 1, 2, 3, 4, 5, 6, 7, 8, 9]
```

```
# condition for the for loop

for i in list:

    print("Welcome!")
```

Output:

```
Welcome!
Welcome!
Welcome!
Welcome!
Welcome!
Welcome!
Welcome!
Welcome!
Welcome!
Welcome!
```

In the given example, we created a list containing ten items. The for loop printed the word "Welcome!" for each item in the list.

Range()

In Python, **range()** is a function that allows us to create a list of numbers in sequence. Instead of creating a list with ten numbers we could use **range(10)** to achieve the same result.

Let's rework the aforementioned code using the **range()** function:

```
for i in range(10):

    print("Welcome!")
```

Output:

```
Welcome!
Welcome!
Welcome!
Welcome!
Welcome!
Welcome!
Welcome!
Welcome!
Welcome!
Welcome!
```

As observed, the **range()** function offers a more efficient way to iterate with the **for** loop.

For loop with else

The **for** loop can also include an additional **else** block. This block executes when the operations in the **for** loop exhaust and the loop terminates naturally, without any interruptions. An interruption can occur using a **break** statement, which stops a loop. If a loop is terminated using **break**, the **else** block is bypassed.

The example below showcases the use of the **else** clause in tandem with a **for** loop.

```
for i in range(5):

    print("Item",i)

else:

    print("No items left")
```

Output:

```
Item 0
Item 1
Item 2
Item 3
Item 4
No items left
```

While loop

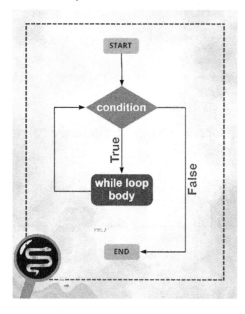

The **while** loop runs as long as its associated condition remains **True**. In essence, it executes statements while its condition holds.

The syntax is the following:

```
while experssion:

    statement(s)
```

Let's replicate the "Welcome!" printout using a **while** loop this time and analyze the distinctions between the two loop types:

```
# creating variable counter

count = 0



# condition for the while loop
```

```
while (count < 10):

    print("Welcome!")


    # increasing the value of count by 1 each iteration

    count = count + 1
```

Output:

```
Welcome!
Welcome!
Welcome!
Welcome!
Welcome!
Welcome!
Welcome!
Welcome!
Welcome!
Welcome!
```

In the provided code, the test expression will remain **True** until the **count** variable remains < 10. The loop increments the **count** variable by 1 during each iteration. Execution halts once the **count** hits 9.

While loop with else

Similar to **for** loops, **while** loops can also be accompanied by an additional **else** block. In a **while** loop, the code block is executed until the condition remains **True**. However, with the **else** block in place, the **else** portion of the **while** loop gets executed if no interruptions occur and the loop condition becomes **False**.

If the **while** loop is prematurely terminated using a **break** statement (which we'll discuss later), the **else** block is ignored.

Below, we illustrate the use of **else** with a **while** loop.

```
count = 0


while (count < 5):

    print("Loop body!")

    count = count + 1

else:

    print("\nElse body!")
```

Output:

```
Loop body!
Loop body!
Loop body!
Loop body!
Loop body!

Else body!
```

We utilize the variable **count** to print "loop body" five times.

On the sixth iteration, when the **while** condition turns **False**, the **else** section is executed, printing "else body".

Nested loops

Python also supports nested loops, where one loop can be placed within another.

Nested for loops have the following sintax:

```
for item in iterator:

    for item in iterator:

        statements(s)

        statements(s)
```

And here's the syntax for nested **while** loops:

```
while expression:

    while expression:

        statement(s)

        statement(s)
```

Let's explore some examples of printing patterns using these nested loops in Python.

```python
# outer loop

for i in range(1, 7):


    # inner loop

    for j in range(1, i+1):

        print("*", end = "")

    print('')
```

Output:

```
*
* *
* * *
* * * *
* * * * *
* * * * * *
* * * * * * *
```

```python
rows = 7

i = 0


# outer loop

while i <= rows:

    j = 1


    # inner loop

    while j <= i:

        print("*", end=" ")

        j = j + 1


    i = i + 1

    print('')
```

Output:

```
*
*  *
*  *  *
*  *  *  *
*  *  *  *  *
*  *  *  *  *  *
*  *  *  *  *  *  *
```

Python loop control statements

Loop control statements alter the flow of code and so the execution at the end will be different from its typical sequence. These statements allow for actions like skipping an iteration or prematurely ending loop execution. In Python we have the following loop control statements:

- **break**
- **continue**
- **pass**

Break statement

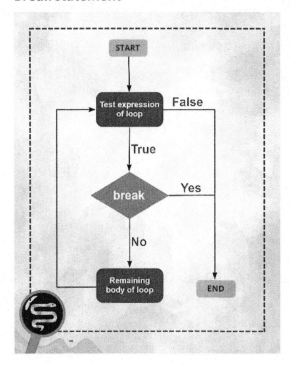

The **break** statement halts loop execution based on a specified condition and transfers control out of the loop. When applied within a nested loop, **break** terminates only the innermost loop.

Let's analyze how the break statement functions within a for loop:

```
# break statement inside the for loop

for letters in "Hello World!":

    if letters == "o":

        break

    print(letters)


print("\nThe end!")
```

Output:

```
H
e
l
l

The end!
```

Note that the output ceased displaying letters from "Hello World!" after the letter "o" due to the **break** statement.

Continue statement

The **continue** statement skips a segment of the loop's body and directly proceeds to the next iteration.

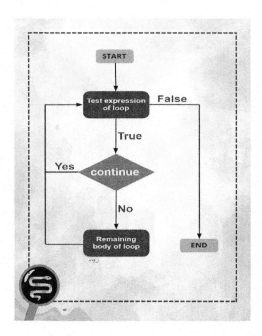

This example demonstrates the continue statement's effect within a for loop:

```
# continue statement inside the for loop

for letters in "Hello World!":

    if letters == "o":

        continue

    print(letters)



print("\nThe end!")
```

Output:

```
H
e
l
l

W
r
l
d
!
```

The end!

Note that the output includes all letters from "Hello World!" except for "o", which was skipped due to the **continue** statement.

Pass statement

The **pass** statement allows us to craft syntactically valid (yet operationally empty) loop bodies, preventing errors. Consider a scenario where we have an incomplete loop that's still under development. An empty loop body would trigger an error; thus, to bypass such situations, we employ the **pass** statement to create a non-operative body.

Now let's see how it works:

```python
# pass statement inside the for loop

for letters in "Hello World!":

    if letters == "o":

        pass


print("The end!")
```

Output:

```
The end!
```

Only the final portion (the **print** function) gets executed. The **for** loop, despite being empty, doesn't generate any errors due to the **pass** statement.

Chapter 8 - Python Conditional Statements

Every day, we make decisions leading to subsequent actions. Similarly, in programming, we must make decisions determining the program's execution path.

This chapter delves into conditional statements, detailing their syntax and use. We will also explore examples illustrating these statements in action.

Conditional statements, often termed decision statements, determine the execution of a specific code block – everything depends on the condition set: is it true or false? In Python, decision-making can be achieved using:

● **if** statements ● **if-else** statements ● **elif** statements ● **Nested if** and **if-else** constructs ● **elif** ladder

if statement

If statements represent the most basic decision-making construct. When the condition is consiered **True**, the code lines within the **if** statement get executed.

"if" statement syntax:

```
if test expression:

    statement
```

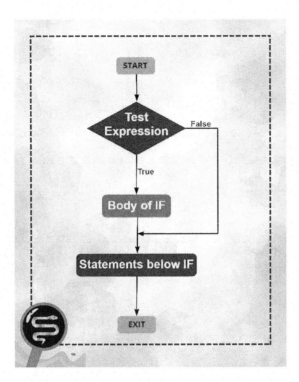

Let's exemplify this with some practice:

```
# assigning a value -9 to num

num = -9


# 'if body' to check if num is less than 10

if (num < 10):

    print(num,"is smaller than 10")



print("This statement will always be executed")
```

Output:

```
-9 is smaller than 10
This statement will always be executed
```

if-else statement

The **if-else** construct facilitates executing either the **True** or **False** branch of a condition. If the condition is considered **True**, then the **if** block is executed; the **else** block is only triggered when the condition is **False**.

"if-else" statement syntax:

if "test expression":

   statement

else:

   statement

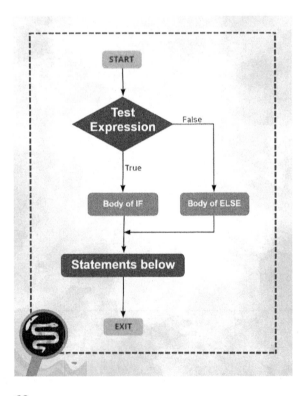

Let's enhance our prior example by integrating the **else** construct:

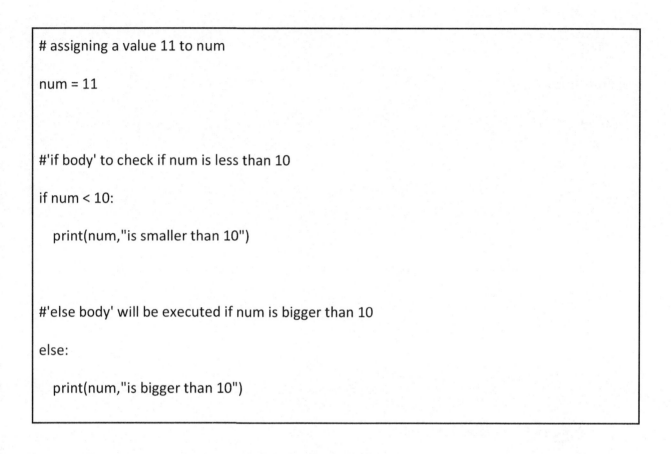

```
# assigning a value 11 to num

num = 11


#'if body' to check if num is less than 10

if num < 10:

    print(num,"is smaller than 10")


#'else body' will be executed if num is bigger than 10

else:

    print(num,"is bigger than 10")
```

Output:

```
11 is bigger than 10
```

elif statement

The **elif** statement evaluates multiple conditions when the initial condition is **False**. It functions similarly to **if-else**, but whereas **else** doesn't assess conditions, **elif** does.

"else" statement syntax:

```
if test expression 1:
```

```
    statement

elif test expression 2:

    statement

elif test expression 3:

    statement

. . .

else:

    statement
```

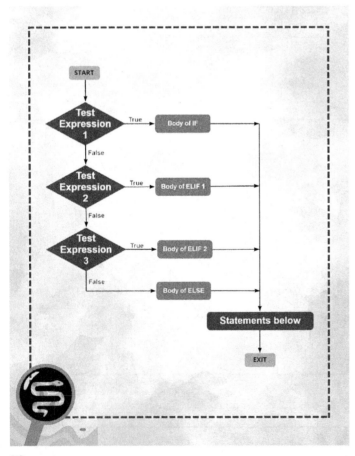

Let's explore how **if-elif-else** statements operate:

```python
# assigning a value 11 to num

num = 0

#'if body' to check if num is less than 0

if num < 0:

    print(num,"is negative number")

# 'elif body' will be executed if num is equal to 0

elif num == 0:

    print(num,"is equal to zero")

#'else body' will be executed if 'if body' is false

else:

    print(num,"is positive number")
```

Output:

```
0 is equal to zero
```

Nested statements

This means that an **if** or **if-else** statement resides within another **if** or **if-else** construct. This enables the evaluation of multiple conditions within a program.

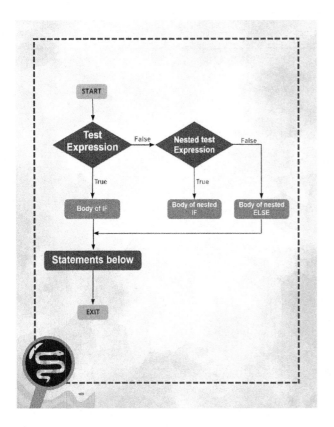

Here's an example of **nested if** statements.

```
# assigning a value 20 to the variable num

num = 20



# checking if num is less than 25

if num < 25:

    print(num, "is less than 25")



    # nested if

    if num == 15:
```

```
    print ("Num is 15")

  elif num == 20:

    print("Num is 10")

  elif num == 10:

    print("Num is 5")

  elif num < 10:

    print("Num is less than 5")
```

Output:

```
20 is less than 25
Num is 10
```

One-line conditional statements

In Python, it's possible to construct "if", "if-else", and "elif" statements in a single line, bypassing the need for indentation.

For example, the simplest if statement looks like this:

```
if expression: statement
```

However, it is possible to add several statements separated by semicolon:

```
if expression: first_statement; second_statement; third_statement; ...; statement_n

elif expression: first_statement; second_statement; third_statement; ...; statement_n

else: first_statement; second_statement; third_statement; ...; statement_n
```

Let's try rewriting the above code with single-line conditional statements. Though single-line conditionals can make code concise, they might compromise readability, especially with complex conditions.

```
# one-line conditional statements

num = 20


if num < 25: print(num, "is less than 25")

if num == 15: print ("Num is 15")

elif num == 20: print("Num is 10")

elif num == 10: print("Num is 5")

elif num < 10: print("Num is less than 5")
```

Output:

```
20 is less than 25
Num is 10
```

As you can see, the output is the same.

Multiple conditions in if statements

We can include a solitary condition within an **if** statement or assess multiple conditions simultaneously using the 'AND' or 'OR' operators, or both.

- With 'AND', both conditions must be True for the statement to execute. The evaluation stops if the first condition is False. If the first is True but the second is False, the overall statement is False.

- With 'OR', at least one condition must be True for execution. If the first condition is True, the statement executes immediately, bypassing the second condition. If the first is False, the second condition is checked. The statement results in False only if both conditions are False.

Consider the examples below to better understand the concept. In the first example, the "age" variable is assessed against two conditions: it should be greater than 18 but also less than 30.

```
age = 18

if age >= 18 and age <= 30:

    print("Welcome!")

  if age == 18:

      print("Please, can you show us your ID card?")

else:

    print("Sorry, we can't let you enter!")
```

Output:
```
Welcome!
Please, can you show us your ID card?
```

Now let's consider another example employing the **OR** operator: you'll observe that more than two conditions can be applied. The end results, despite variations in the code, remain consistent.

```python
age = 18

if age > 18 or age == 18 and age <= 30:

    print("Welcome!\nCan you show us your ID card?")

else:

    print("Sorry, you can't enter!")
```

Output:

```
Welcome!
Can you show us your ID card?
```

Chapter 9 - Python Functions

In this chapter we will learn about the different Python functions and the difference between built-in and user-defined ones. We will delve deep into user-defined functions, look at different mechanisms for passing arguments, and learn how to return results from our functions. Also, we will understand the benefits of using user-defined functions and the best practices to follow.

In Python, a function consists of a group of related statements that carry out a specific task, which can be computational, logical, or evaluative. Functions come in two types: built-in and user-defined. The idea is to group a number of often-repeated processes and create a function instead of writing the same code repeatedly. This makes the program more concise, non-repetitive, and organized.

User-defined vs. built-in functions in Python

Built-in functions are already integrated into Python's libraries and can be used directly. These functions cannot be altered by users. For example, 'print()' is a built-in function that produces output on the screen.

User-defined functions, on the other hand, are functions we define in our programs. They can be called wherever desired and modified if necessary. To create a user-defined function we will use the 'def' keyword, specifying the function name. Then, we can call it through its name, followed by parentheses that contain all the required parameters.

Here is the syntax:

```
def function_name (parameters):

    statements

    return expression
```

Let's examine the different components:

- **def**: The keyword signifying the start of the function.

- **function_name**: An identifier for the function's name.

- **parameters**: An optional comma-separated list indicating the values we want to pass to the function.

- **::** A colon, marking the end of the function header.

- **statements**: These represent the real body of the function.

- **return expression**: This an optional statement, used of we want to return a value from the function.

A basic user-defined function could be the following:

```
def function():

    print("It's a user-defined function which prints this message")


function()
```

Output:

```
It's a user-defined function which prints this message
```

Function arguments

Arguments provide data to a function, enabling varied behavior between calls. Arguments are given within parentheses when calling a function, separated by commas. Even if a function has no parameters, it must still have parentheses, even if empty.

We can use various types of arguments in a function call:

- Default arguments
- Required arguments
- Keyword arguments
- Variable-length arguments

Default arguments

Default arguments ensure that if an argument isn't provided a value when the function is called, this function will use a default value.

The code below explains the concept of default arguments:

```python
# definign a function 'info'

def info(name, age = 20 ):

    print("Name:", name)

    print("Age:", age)

    return


# calling 'info' function giving value to age

info(age = 18, name = "Alex" )


# calling info function where age has default value

info(name = "Astrid")
```

Output:

```
Name: Alex
Age: 18
Name: Astrid
Age: 20
```

Required arguments

Arguments that must be passed to a function in the specified positional order are known as required arguments. The count of arguments used when calling the function must be identical to the number of arguments defined in the function's declaration.

```python
# definig a function passing arguments 'num','item','price'

def function(num, item, price):

    print(f'{num} {item} cost ${price}')



# specifying values for arguments

function(100, 'socks', 200)
```

Output:

```
100 socks cost $200
```

Keyword arguments

In a function call utilizing named arguments, the caller specifies each parameter by its designated name. Unlike required arguments, we can skip or rearrange the arguments.

For instance, the previously defined function can be called using keyword arguments:

```python
# calling arguments by keywords

def function(num, item, price):

    print(f'{num} {item} cost ${price}')
```

```
function(item ='socks', price = 200, num = 100)
```

Output:

        `100 socks cost $200`

Variable-length arguments

There are times when we might call a function with more arguments than initially declared. These arguments aren't explicitly stated in the function declaration. Special characters allow us to pass a varying number of parameters to a function. These characters are:

- *args (for non-keyword arguments)
- **kwargs (for keyword arguments)

```
def function_name(formal_args, *var_args_tuple ):

    function_body

    return expression
```

Let's explore a basic example utilizing variable-length arguments:

```
def function(*argv):

  for arg in argv:

    print(arg)
```

```
function("Hello","Guys!", "\nWhat", "are", "you", "doing?")
```

Output:

```
Hello
Guys!

What
are
you
doing?
```

Docstrings

Immediately after the function header, we have the docstring, short for "documentation string": it explains the function's purpose. We can create a docstring using triple quotes. It's good practice to use a docstring, even if optional.

This string is available to us as a __doc__ attribute of a function.

Below is the syntax for the output of a function's docstring:

```
print(function_name.__doc__)
```

Here below you can see an example of adding Docstring to a function:

```
def odd_even(n):

    """Our goal with this function is to verify if a number is even or odd"""



    if (n % 2 == 0):

        print(n, " is even")

    else:
```

```
    print(n, " is odd")



print(odd_even.__doc__)
```

Return statement in Python functions

The return statement in a function serves to conclude the function's execution, transfer control back to the caller, and deliver a specified value or data item. The syntax is as follows:

```
return [expression_list]
```

This statement can evaluate expressions and return their values. If no expression is associated with the return or if the return statement is absent, the function will return a **None** object.

Let's consider an example of user-defined functions using the return statement:

```
def square(num):

    return num**2



print("Square of 2 is",square(2))

print("Square of -3 is",square(-3))
```

Output:

```
    Square of 2 is 4
    Square of -3 is 9
```

In the provided example, the return statement computes the square of a given number.

Chapter 10 - Python Modules

A Python module is essentially a file containing Python code, including definitions and statements. It can encompass functions, classes, and variables, and might also contain executable code. Organizing related pieces of code within a module enhances its readability and functionality. Python is renowned for its vast collection of built-in modules, so we can often avoid writing everything from zero; instead, we can call a module to leverage its functionality.

Different ways to importing module

All built-in modules are readily available without installation. However, if we want to use a module not included with the standard Python package, it must be installed. One straightforward way to install a module is using the **pip** command. For instance, the **pandas** module can be installed with **pip** as demonstrated below.

```
pip install pandas
```

Let's delve into various ways of importing modules.

The import keyword is usually the preferred choice to import a module. For example, let's say that we want to install the **math** module and perform some operations.

```python
# import standard math module
import math


# finding the square root
root = math.sqrt(9)


print(root)
```

Output:

```
3.0
```

As you can see, we obtained the square root of the specified number.

Another approach to import modules is via the **as** keyword. When a module's name is lengthy or not intuitive, we can alias it using **as**.

```
# importing module using as keyword
import math as m


# finding the square root
root = m.sqrt(9)


print(root)
```

Output:

```
3.0
```

Notice, after importing the module as **m**, this alias encompasses all module functionalities. So, instead of repeatedly invoking the module's name, we can simply use **m**.

At times, we might only need specific methods from a module rather than the entire module. This can be achieved with the **from** keyword, as shown below.

```
# from key word
from math import sqrt


# finding root
root = sqrt(9)


print(root)
```

Output:

```
3.0
```

To import every element from a module, including variables and names, we use the asterisk symbol:

```python
# importing everything
from math import *


# pi value
PI = pi


print(pi)
```

Output:

3.141592653589793

We were able to display the value of pi since it's defined within the **math** module, and we imported everything from that module.

Creating a Module in Python

Creating a module in Python is quite simple. First, create a new Python file named **module.py**.

```
☐  ☐ module.py
```

As you can see, we have created an empty Python file. Now, open the file and write the following code:

```python
# Defining a function
def sample():
    print('This is our sample module')
```

Once the function is defined, save the file as **module.py**. Subsequently, in another Python file, import the module to access the **sample()** function:

```
# importing the module
import module as md


# accessing the sample function
md.sample()
```

Output:

```
This is our sample module
```

Upon importing the module, we successfully accessed the function contained within.

Now you can experiment by importing the module using the different techniques we explored in this chapter.

Chapter 11 - Files in Python

Sometimes, we need to manage data across separate files or save data to different files. For such tasks, familiarity with file handling in Python is essential.

A file is a crucial data item stored on a computer. Each file has a distinct filename and file extension. Throughout this book, we'll predominantly work with .txt file extensions.

Understanding the open() function

The **open()** function in Python is used to access files. The file's path should be passed to the **open()** function as a string.

The syntax for opening a file in Python using the **open()** method is as follows:

```
with open('<PATH>','<MODE>') as <FILE_OBJECT>:
```

This function will return a FILE_OBJECT that represents our file, and can be assigned to any variable.

There are various modes available for file access:

Mode	Description
x	This will generate a new blank file. We cannot perform this operation in case the file already exists.
r	It will only open the file in read-only mode (the file must already exist)
w	It will open a file for writing, and in case it does not exist, it is created; otherwise, it is truncated.
a	If the file already exists, it is preserved, and the additional data you provide will be appended to what is already there. Also in this case, if no file exists, it is created.

r +	You will be allowed to read the file and also write on it; the cursor is put at the beginning. You will see an error if no file exists.
w+	Both reading and writing also in this case. If the file is already present, it will be truncated and overwritten; otherwise, it will be created.
a+	Reading and writing again. If the file is already present, it will be preserved and the data you want to add will be appended to what is already there. If no file exists, it will be created.

How to create an empty file in Python
We have several methods exist to generate an empty file.

The first method utilizes the **pathlib** module. Pathlib offers an object-oriented interface to the filesystem, providing a more intuitive, platform-independent, and Pythonic way to engage with it. Here's how you can work with **pathlib**:

```
from pathlib import Path

Path('file.txt').touch()
```

This action creates an empty file in the designated directory:

☐ 🗎 file.txt

☐ 🗎 module.py

Another method is the **open()** function with the 'x' mode, which will create a new empty file:

```
with open('FILE.txt', 'x') as file_object:
    pass
```

If executed again, it would return an error since the file has already been created:

```
FileExistsError                        Traceback (mo
st recent call last)
/tmp/ipykernel_4871/1328198799.py in <module>
----> 1 with open('FILE.txt', 'x') as file_object:
      2     pass

FileExistsError: [Errno 17] File exists: 'FILE.txt'
```

How to write to a file

If your goal is to write to a file, invoke the **open()** method with the 'w' mode, indicating that data should be written to the file. If the specified file is not present, this mode will generate a new one. If the file already exists, the content will be overwritten. Here's how you can write to a file:

```
#opening the file in writing mode

with open('file.txt', 'w') as file_object:


    # adding content to the file
    file_object.write("Writing the first content to the file\n")
```

The **write()** method facilitates writing to the file. If we open the file, we will see the following:

```
1  Writing the first content to the file
2
```

Let's write the content in multiple lines:

```
#opening the file in writing mode

with open('file.txt', 'w') as file_object:
```

90

```
# adding content to the file
file_object.write("Writing the \nfirst content \nto the file\n")
```

Output:

```
1  Writing the
2  first content
3  to the file
4
```

As you can see, the content is now written in multiple lines.

How to read content from a file?

The **read()** method allows us to extract content from a file. After opening the file, the data can be stored in a variable:

```
# Opening the file in reading mode
file_object =  open('file.txt', 'r')


# storing the content in variable
content = file_object.read()


# print the content
print(content)
```

Output:

```
Writing the
first content
to the file
```

At times, you might wish to read only specific lines from the file; this task is achievable using a **for** loop:

```
# Opening the file in reading mode
with open('file.txt', 'r') as file_object:

    # for loop to acces each line
    for line in file_object:
        print(line)
```

Output:

```
Writing the

first content

to the file
```

As you can see, each line has been printed using the **for** loop.

You can experiment by opening the file in various modes and exploring each mode's practical applications.

Chapter 12 - Error Handling in Python

The try-except block

In Python, error handling refers to the practice of anticipating and addressing potential error conditions during your program's runtime. This is vital when your program interacts with external resources, such as databases or network connections, which might not always be available.

Error handling in Python uses try-except blocks:

```
try:
  # code that may raise an exception
except ExceptionType:
  # code that will handle the exception
```

The try block contains code that might trigger an exception, and the except block contains the code that addresses the exception if it arises. The ExceptionType is the specific exception you aim to catch and manage. For instance, if you're reading a file and want to address the scenario where the file is missing, you can use a try-except block as follows:

```
try:
  f = open("myfile.txt")
  # code that works with the file
except IOError:
  print("Error: Could not find file or read data")
```

In this example, the try block attempts to open the file called "myfile.txt". If the file isn't present, or the program lacks read permissions, an IOError exception will arise. The except block will then be executed, displaying an error message.

Handling Multiple Exceptions Using the except Keyword

In Python, the try and except keywords manage exceptions: in the try block there is code that might trigger an exception, while in the except block there is code that responds when an exception occurs. You can address several exceptions in one except block by listing the exception names separated by commas or in distinct blocks:

```python
try:
    # code that may throw an exception
    x = int(input("Enter a number: "))
    y = 1 / x
except ValueError:
    # code to be executed if a ValueError is raised
    print("You must enter a valid number.")
except ZeroDivisionError:
    # code to be executed if a ZeroDivisionError is raised
    print("You cannot divide by zero.")
```

In this instance, the try block prompts the user for a number and then tries to divide 1 by that number. A ValueError is triggered if the user inputs a value that isn't an integer. A ZeroDivisionError is triggered if the user inputs 0. The except block manages these exceptions individually.

You can also use the except keyword without specifying any exception type to catch all exceptions from the try block. Still, it's generally better to specify which exceptions you're targeting. This specificity enables more precise error handling.

```python
try:
    # code that may throw an exception
    x = int(input("Enter a number: "))
    y = 1 / x
```

```
except ValueError:

    # code to be executed if a ValueError is raised

    print("You must enter a valid number.")

except ZeroDivisionError:

    # code to be executed if a ZeroDivisionError is raised

    print("You cannot divide by zero.")

except:

    # code to be executed if any other exception is raised

    print("An unexpected error occurred.")
```

In this example, the except block at the end will catch any exception that is not explicitly handled by the other except blocks; this is useful as a catch-all error handling mechanism, however, it's generally better practice to specify which exceptions you're aiming to handle

Using the else Keyword in try-except Statements

The else keyword could be used in try-except statements to designate a portion of code that should run if no exceptions arise during the try block's execution.

Here is an example of how to use the else keyword in a try-except statement:

```
try:

    # code that may raise an exception

    result = 10 / 0

except ZeroDivisionError:

    # code to handle ZeroDivisionError exception

    print("Division by zero is not allowed")

else:

    # code to be executed if no exception occurs

    print("Result:", result)
```

If you run this example, the output will be "Division by zero is not allowed" because the ZeroDivisionError exception is triggered and managed by the except block.

On the other hand, if the try block does not raise any exception, the code in the else block will be executed. For example:

```python
try:
    # code that may raise an exception
    result = 10 / 5
except ZeroDivisionError:
    # code to handle ZeroDivisionError exception
    print("Division by zero is not allowed")
else:
    # code to be executed if no exception occurs
    print("Result:", result)
```

In this case the else block runs, leading to the output "Result: 2". It's important to note that the else block only runs if the try block doesn't raise an exception. If an exception arises and is managed by an except block, the else block remains unexecuted.

The finally Block in try-except Statements
The finally block in Python's exception handling mechanism always runs, regardless of whether the try block produces an exception. It's helpful for cleanup tasks, like closing files or relinquishing resources. Here is an example:

```python
try:
    f = open("myfile.txt")
    # code that works with the file
except IOError:
    print("Error: Could not find file or read data")
finally:
    f.close()
```

In this example, the try block attempts to open "myfile.txt" and process its contents. If the file is absent or the program lacks read permissions, an IOError exception is triggered. The except block manages this exception, displaying an error message. No matter whether an exception is triggered, the finally block always executes to close the file.

You can also use a finally block without an except block:

```
try:
    f = open("myfile.txt")
    # code that works with the file
finally:
    f.close()
```

In this case, the finally block still executes, even if no exceptions arise in the try block.

It is important to use the finally block when working with resources like files or database connections to ensure they're closed or released after use. This approach prevents resource leaks and guarantees your program cleans up after operations.

Here's another example of using a finally block to release a database connection:

```
try:
    # code that accesses the database
except DatabaseError:
    # code that handles the database error
finally:
    connection.close()
```

In this scenario, the finally block always executes to close the database connection, regardless of whether an exception occurs during database access. It's also possible to use a finally block alongside an else block:

```
try:
```

```
    f = open("myfile.txt")
    # code that works with the file
except IOError:
    print("Error: Could not find file or read data")
else:
    print("File opened successfully")
finally:
    f.close()
```

In this setup, the else block only executes if no exceptions are raised in the try block, and the finally block always executes.

Chapter 13 - Python standard libraries

Python is equipped with a comprehensive standard library that facilitates various common programming tasks, including connecting to web servers, manipulating files, and processing data. These libraries seamlessly integrate with the language, ensuring user-friendly interactions. The Python standard library is structured into several submodules. Each submodule comprises a set of interconnected functions and classes. A few of the most frequently used standard libraries are:

1. **math**: Offers mathematical functions such as sin, cos, and sqrt.

2. **statistics**: Contains statistical functions like mean, median, and standard deviation.

3. **random**: Equipped with functions for generating pseudo-random numbers.

4. **string**: Provides tools for string operations, ranging from formatting to manipulation.

5. **re**: Facilitates support for regular expressions used for pattern matching within strings.

6. **collections**: Houses specialized container datatypes like dictionaries, lists, and sets.

Beyond these foundational libraries, Python also boasts an extensive range of libraries tailored for specific tasks such as file management, data manipulation, and OS interactions.

math - Mathematical Functions
The **math** module, an intrinsic part of Python's library suite, serves a plethora of mathematical functions and constants. Here are some prominent functions from the **math** module:

- **math.ceil(x)**: Yields the smallest integer $\geq x$.

- **math.floor(x)**: Provides the largest integer $\leq x$.

- **math.factorial(x)**: Computes the factorial of x.

- **math.gcd(x, y)**: Determines the greatest common divisor of x and y.

- **math.isqrt(x)**: Extracts the integer part of x's square root.

- **math.sqrt(x)**: Calculates the square root of x.

- **math.isclose(x, y, *, rel_tol=1e-09, abs_tol=0.0)**: Checks if x and y are approximately equal.

This module also showcases mathematical constants like **math.pi** and **math.e**.

Here is an example of using some of the functions in the math module:

```
import math

# Calculate the square root of 25

x = math.sqrt(25)

print(x)


# Calculate the ceiling of 3.7

y = math.ceil(3.7)

print(y)


# Calculate the factorial of 5

z = math.factorial(5)

print(z)

# Check if the values 3.14 and math.pi are close to each other

a = math.isclose(3.14, math.pi)

print(a)
```

Output:

```
5.0

4

120

True
```

Statistics - Mathematical Statistics Functions

The **statistics** module, inherent to Python, presents functions tailored for statistical computations. Here's a snapshot of its offerings:

- **statistics.mean(data)**: Computes the average of the data.

- **statistics.median(data)**: Identifies the median value.

- **statistics.mode(data)**: Pinpoints the most frequently occurring value.

- **statistics.stdev(data)**: Measures data's standard deviation.

- **statistics.variance(data)**: Evaluates the variance.

Here is an example of using some of the functions in the statistics module:

```
import statistics


# Calculate the mean of a list of numbers

data = [1, 2, 3, 4, 5]

mean = statistics.mean(data)

print(mean)

```

```
# Calculate the median of a list of numbers

median = statistics.median(data)

print(median)


# Calculate the mode of a list of numbers

mode = statistics.mode(data)

print(mode)


# Calculate the standard deviation of a list of numbers

stdev = statistics.stdev(data)

print(stdev)


# Calculate the variance of a list of numbers

variance = statistics.variance(data)

print(variance)
```

Output:

```
3.0

3.0

1

1.5811388300841898

2.5
```

random - Pseudo-Random Number Generation

Python's **random** module furnishes functions for producing pseudo-random numbers. These numbers, derived from mathematical algorithms, aren't truly random but suffice for numerous applications, such as list shuffling or unique ID creation. Key functions include:

- **random.random()**: Generates a random float between [0.0, 1.0).

- **random.uniform(a, b)**: Returns a random float within [a, b).

- **random.randint(a, b)**: Outputs a random integer spanning [a, b].

- **random.choice(sequence)**: Picks a random element from the sequence.

- **random.shuffle(sequence)**: Shuffles the sequence elements.

Here is an example of using some of the functions in the random module:

```python
import random


# Generate a random float between 0 and 1

x = random.random()

print(x)

# Generate a random float between 10 and 20

y = random.uniform(10, 20)

print(y)

# Generate a random integer between 1 and 10

z = random.randint(1, 10)

print(z)

# Choose a random element from a list
```

```
data = [1, 2, 3, 4, 5]

element = random.choice(data)

print(element)


# Shuffle a list

random.shuffle(data)

print(data)
```

Output:

```
0.5435342345235

16.5435342345235

6

3

[2, 5, 1, 4, 3]
```

string - String Operations

The **string** module, inherent to Python, is geared for string handling. A few notable functions are:

- **string.ascii_letters**: Lists all ASCII letters.

- **string.digits**: Comprises all ASCII digits.

- **string.hexdigits**: Enumerates all hexadecimal ASCII digits.

- **string.punctuation**: Contains all ASCII punctuation symbols.

- **string.capwords(s, sep=None)**: Capitalizes words within a string.

- **string.maketrans(x[, y[, z]])**: Returns a translation table for Unicode character translation.

Here is an example of using some of the functions in the string module:

```
import string


# Check if a character is an ASCII letter

char = 'a'

result = char in string.ascii_letters

print(result)# Check if a character is an ASCII digit

char = '5'

result = char in string.digits

print(result)


# Check if a character is an ASCII hexadecimal digit

char = 'f'

result = char in string.hexdigits

print(result)

# Capitalize the words in a string

s = 'this is a test string'

result = string.capwords(s)

print(result)
```

```
# Format a string using a mapping

template = '{name} is {age} years old'

mapping = {'name': 'John', 'age': 30}

result = template.format_map(mapping)

print(result)
```

Output:

```
 True

True

True

This Is A Test String

John is 30 years old
```

re - Regular Expression Operations

Python's built-in **re** module offers a suite of functions tailored for regular expression operations. Regular expressions serve as a potent mechanism for detecting and extrapolating string patterns. Some salient functions within the **re** module are:

- **re.compile(pattern)**: Converts a regular expression pattern into a regex object.

- **re.match(pattern, string)**: Endeavors to apply the pattern at the outset of the string.

- **re.search(pattern, string)**: Traverses the string to pinpoint the pattern's initial occurrence.

- **re.findall(pattern, string)**: Detects every instance of the pattern within the string.

- **re.sub(pattern, repl, string)**: Modifies each instance of the pattern in the string with a replacement string.

Here is an example of using some of the functions in the re module:

```python
import re

# Compile a regular expression pattern

pattern = re.compile(r'\d+')


# Match the pattern to the beginning of a string

string = '123abc456'

result = pattern.match(string)

print(result.group())


# Search for the first occurrence of the pattern in the string

result = pattern.search(string)

print(result.group())


# Find all occurrences of the pattern in the string

result = pattern.findall(string)

print(result)


# Replace all occurrences of the pattern in the string

result = pattern.sub('000', string)
```

```
print(result)
```

Output:

```
'123'

'123'

['123', '456']

'000abc000'
```

collections - Container Data Types

The inherent **collections** module in Python presents specialized container data types. These types facilitate more efficient and user-friendly data storage and manipulation compared to native Python data types like lists and dictionaries. Some prominent container data types from the **collections** module are:

- **collections.Counter**: An extension of the dictionary, it tallies item occurrences within an iterable.

- **collections.OrderedDict**: An extended dictionary that preserves the sequence of key additions.

- **collections.defaultdict**: A dictionary derivative that assigns a default value for absent keys.

- **collections.deque**: A bidirectional queue supporting rapid insertions and deletions from both extremities.

- **collections.namedtuple**: An extended tuple permitting element accessibility by name alongside index.

Here is an example of using some of the container data types in the collections module:

```python
import collections


# Count the occurrences of items in a list

data = ['a', 'b', 'c', 'a', 'b', 'b']

counter = collections.Counter(data)

print(counter)


# Maintain the order in which keys are added to a dictionary

odict = collections.OrderedDict()

odict['a'] = 1

odict['b'] = 2

odict['c'] = 3

print(odict)


# Provide a default value for missing keys in a dictionary

ddict = collections.defaultdict(int)

ddict['a'] = 1

ddict['b'] = 2

print(ddict['c'])


# Use a double-ended queue
```

```
deque = collections.deque()

deque.append('a')

deque.append('b')

deque.appendleft('c')

print(deque)


# Access elements of a tuple by name as well as by index

Person = collections.namedtuple('Person', ['name', 'age'])

person = Person(name='John', age=30)

print(person.name)

print(person[1])
```

Output:

```
Counter({'b': 3, 'a': 2, 'c': 1})

OrderedDict([('a', 1), ('b', 2), ('c', 3)])

0

deque(['c', 'a', 'b'])

'John'

30
```

Chapter 14 - TensorFlow

TensorFlow is an open-source software library tailor-made for machine learning and artificial intelligence. Conceived and nurtured by Google, it's made publicly accessible under the Apache 2.0 license. TensorFlow empowers developers to architect machine learning models and then seamlessly deploy them across varied environments, including on-premises setups and cloud platforms.

A major attribute of TensorFlow is its adaptability to run across diverse platforms — from traditional CPUs to more advanced GPUs and even TPUs (Tensor Processing Units). This universality allows developers to exploit the prowess of specialized hardware, maintaining consistency in their codebase.

Supporting TensorFlow's growing stature is its thriving community, which ensures a plethora of online resources for learners and enthusiasts.

Some of the key features of TensorFlow include:

- **Flexibility**: With TensorFlow, a myriad of architectures and algorithms can be utilized for both conventional and deep learning tasks.

- **Efficiency**: Crafted for scalability, TensorFlow ensures swift training, particularly for complex models.

- **Portability**: It's adaptable across various platforms, from PCs to mobile devices.

- **Documentation**: Newcomers will find TensorFlow's comprehensive resources—including guides, API details, and tutorials—particularly helpful.

- **Extensibility**: Custom operations, models, and layers can be defined in TensorFlow, tailoring it to specific requirements. Moreover, its expansive third-party tool ecosystem further augments its capabilities.

Installation and setup

To commence your journey with TensorFlow, initiate its installation on your machine. Leveraging Python's package manager, pip, eases this process. Write in your terminal the following command:

```
pip install tensorflow
```

This fetches the latest TensorFlow version. For a specific version, append the desired number:

```
pip install tensorflow==2.4.0
```

For those wanting to tinker with TensorFlow's source code and wish real-time reflection of modifications, pip's "editable" mode is a boon. To do this, write this code:

```
pip install -e /path/to/TensorFlow/source_code
```

This will install TensorFlow in "editable" mode, meaning that any changes you make to the source code will be reflected immediately.

Once TensorFlow is in your system, you can upload it into your Python code through this import statement:

```
import tensorflow as tf
```

This will import the TensorFlow library into your Python code and give it the alias "tf".

TensorFlow basics

Tensor is a multi-dimensional data array that stands as the foundational data structure in TensorFlow; it is used to represent the data that flows through a TensorFlow computation.

A tensor's key attribute is its shape. The shape encapsulates the number of dimensions it holds and the extent of each of them. For instance, a tensor of shape [3, 4] translates to a 2-dimensional array boasting 3 rows and 4 columns. Meanwhile, a tensor with a shape of [2, 3, 4] signifies a 3-dimensional structure with 2 slices, 3 rows, and 4 columns.

In TensorFlow computations, tensors are used to represent initial data, the intermediate outputs, and the final results. TensorFlow operations accept these tensors as their input and yield tensors as the resulting output. Many of these operations form the backbone of machine learning models, and they can be intertwined in numerous configurations to craft intricate machine learning algorithms.

Sessions and Graphs in TensorFlow

What makes TensorFlow stand out is its ability to conceptualize computations without immediate execution, awaiting an explicit instruction to perform the computation. This might appear perplexing at first. However, this is where TensorFlow's Graph and Session come into play.

- Every computation in TensorFlow is represented by a Graph.

- To execute the computations which are stored in the form of a graph, we need to initialize a session.

So, basically, TensorFlow needs graphs and sessions to store and execute the computations.

The Graph in TensorFlow is not only a simple data structure, but it visually portrays a computational operation: it consists of a set of nodes (representing operations) and edges (representing the input/output relationships between the nodes). It essentially charts out computations ready for execution, potentially across multiple devices or servers. Let's see an example to better understand how to create and use a Graph in TensorFlow:

```
# defining the variables

x = 10

y = 15



# addition using tensorflow
```

```
Summation = tf.add(x, y, name='Add')



# printing the sum

print(Summation)
```

Output:

```
tf.Tensor(25, shape=(), dtype=int32)
```

We get a lot of information as output instead of just an addition of the two numbers. In the code above, the **tf.add()** takes the names of the variables and the operation. In our case, the operation is "Add", which means we want to add the two variables.

In TensorFlow, a Session is a class that represents a connection between the Python program and the C++ runtime that executes TensorFlow operations. A Session object provides method calls to drive the computation by feeding tensors and running the operations defined in a Graph.

```
import tensorflow.compat.v1 as tf

tf.disable_v2_behavior()



# Build a computational graph

a = tf.constant(3.0)

b = tf.constant(4.0)

c = tf.add(a, b)



# Launch the graph in a session

sess = tf.Session()
```

```
# Evaluate the tensor c

print(sess.run(c))


# Close the session to release resources

sess.close()
```

Output:

```
7.0
```

Basic Operations in TensorFlow:

Let's discuss some basic mathematical operations that can be performed between tensors in TensorFlow.

First, let's start by creating some tensors using TensorFlow's **constant()** function:

```
import tensorflow as tf

# Create a 1-dimensional tensor with 3 elements

tensor1 = tf.constant([1, 2, 3])

# Create a 2-dimensional tensor with 2 rows and 3 columns

tensor2 = tf.constant([[1, 2, 3], [4, 5, 6]])
```

Addition:

Using the **add()** function in TensorFlow, you can combine two tensors, yielding a tensor that represents the sum:

```
import tensorflow.compat.v1 as tf

tf.disable_v2_behavior()


# Add tensor1 and tensor2

result = tf.add(tensor1, tensor2)


# Launch the graph in a session

sess = tf.Session()


# Evaluate the tensor c

print(sess.run(result))
```

Output:

```
[[2 4 6]

[5 7 9]]
```

Subtraction:

The **subtract()** function takes two tensors and returns their element-wise difference.

```
import tensorflow.compat.v1 as tf

tf.disable_v2_behavior()

# Add tensor1 and tensor2

result = tf.subtract(tensor1, tensor2)
```

```
# Launch the graph in a session

sess = tf.Session()


# Evaluate the tensor c

print(sess.run(result))
```

Output:

```
[[ 0  0  0]

[-3 -3 -3]]
```


Multiplication:

With the **multiply()** function, element-wise product of two tensors can be obtained.

```
import tensorflow.compat.v1 as tf

tf.disable_v2_behavior()


# Add tensor1 and tensor2

result = tf.multiply(tensor1, tensor2)


# Launch the graph in a session

sess = tf.Session()

# Evaluate the tensor
```

```
print(sess.run(result))
```

Output:

```
[[ 1  4  9]

 [ 4 10 18]]
```

Division:

The **divide()** function allows you to get the quotient of two tensors on an element-wise basis:

```
import tensorflow.compat.v1 as tf

tf.disable_v2_behavior()


# Add tensor1 and tensor2

result = tf.divide(tensor1, tensor2)


# Launch the graph in a session

sess = tf.Session()


# Evaluate the tensor

print(sess.run(result))
```

Output:

```
[[1.  1.  1. ]

 [0.25 0.4  0.5 ]]
```

Creating and training a model

TensorFlow is renowned for its training speed and predictions. To create and train a model in TensorFlow, we follow these straightforward steps:

• **Data Preparation:** Data Preparation: Involves collecting and cleaning data, then splitting it into training, validation, and test datasets.

• **Defining the Model:** This involves selecting a model architecture and articulating the model in TensorFlow using either the layers API or the Keras API.

• **Compiling the Model:** This step requires specifying the loss function and optimizer for training, along with any supplementary metrics to monitor.

• **Model Training:** Entails processing the training data through the model, with the loss function and optimizer adjusting the model's parameters.

• **Model Evaluation:** Consists of testing the model's effectiveness on unseen data to check for overfitting or underfitting.

• **Fine-tuning the Model:** Adjustments and enhancements will be required if the model doesn't meet performance expectations. This could involve tweaking its hyperparameters, modifying its layers, or applying regularization techniques.

Let's suppose we want to create and train a simple model in TensorFlow with the Keras API:

```python
import tensorflow as tf


# Load the MNIST dataset

(x_train, y_train), (x_test, y_test) = tf.keras.datasets.mnist.load_data()


# Normalize the data
```

```python
x_train = x_train / 255.0

x_test = x_test / 255.0


# Build the model

model = tf.keras.Sequential([

  tf.keras.layers.Flatten(input_shape=(28, 28)),

  tf.keras.layers.Dense(128, activation='relu'),

  tf.keras.layers.Dense(10, activation='softmax')

])


# Compile the model

model.compile(optimizer='adam',                loss='sparse_categorical_crossentropy',
metrics=['accuracy'])


# Train the model

model.fit(x_train, y_train, epochs=5)


# Evaluate the model

test_loss, test_acc = model.evaluate(x_test, y_test)

print('Test accuracy:', test_acc)
```

Output:

```
Test accuracy: 0.9748
```

We initially load the MNIST dataset, a collection of images showcasing handwritten digits along with their corresponding labels. Subsequently, we normalize the data by dividing it by 255.0.

We then design a basic model comprising two fully-connected layers. The initial layer boasts 128 units, while the second layer features 10 units, aligning with the 10 classes found within the MNIST dataset.

Next, the model undergoes compilation, where we detail the optimizer and loss function intended for training. For this instance, the Adam optimizer and the sparse categorical cross-entropy loss function are employed.

Following that, the model is trained using the **fit()** method, where we designate the training data and the epoch count. An epoch represents a singular pass through the entirety of the training dataset.

The model's evaluation is based on the test data, after which the test accuracy is displayed.

This is just an example of creating and training a model in TensorFlow using the Keras API. There are many more options and techniques that you can use to fine-tune and optimize your model, including data augmentation, regularization, and hyperparameter tuning.

Chapter 15 - NumPy Module

NumPy is a robust library tailored for numerical operations. It offers capabilities ranging from array creation and manipulation to performing different types of mathematical operations on arrays. Some salient features of NumPy include:

- **Array Creation**: Create arrays in diverse shapes and sizes, initialized with zeros, ones, random values, or specific user values.

- **Array Indexing**: Use standard Python indexing and slicing to access or modify elements or subarrays.

- **Array Operations**: Execute element-wise operations like addition, subtraction, and more. It also supports linear algebra operations, such as matrix multiplication.

- **Array Manipulation**: Reshape, transpose, concatenate arrays, and perform array sorting or searching.

- **Array Broadcasting**: Perform operations on arrays that have different shapes. NumPy's broadcasting stretches the array with a smaller shaper to fit the larger array's shape.

- **Array Statistics**: Compute statistical metrics like mean, median, and standard deviation.

- **Array I/O**: Read and write arrays to/from files and convert arrays between different data formats.

Thanks to its efficient, optimized functions, NumPy stands out as a formidable tool for numerical data processing in Python. In the upcoming sections, we will delve into the intricacies of the NumPy module through hands-on examples.

Installing the NumPy Module

Before using NumPy, ensure its installation. If you skip this step, running a NumPy-based code will yield errors. To install NumPy:

1. Open your terminal.

2. Enter the command: **pip install numpy**

Wait for the installation to complete. Post-installation, verify its success using this command:

```
import numpy as np
```

If no error surfaces, the installation was successful.

Understanding NumPy Array Objects

NumPy's heart lies in its array object, dedicated to storing and manipulating extensive homogeneous data arrays. While reminiscent of Python's native list and tuple, NumPy arrays are optimized for efficiency and offer multidimensionality. You can achieve operations element-wise on these arrays rather than relying on Python's loop constructs.

Create a NumPy array using the **numpy.array** function:

```
import numpy as np


# Create a 1-dimensional array

a = np.array([1, 2, 3, 4])


# Create a 2-dimensional array

b = np.array([[1, 2], [3, 4]])
```

Note that NumPy arrays have an immutable size. To alter an array's size, you'd have to create a fresh array and transfer the data.

Arrays come with a designated data type, defining the nature of the data they hold. NumPy accommodates various data types, such as integers, floating-point values, and complex numbers.

You can define an array's data type when creating it, or NumPy can deduce it based on the data provided to the numpy.array function.

```
import numpy as np

# Create an array with a specific data type

a = np.array([1, 2, 3, 4], dtype=np.float64)

# Create an array and let NumPy infer the data type

b = np.array([1, 2, 3, 4])
```

Indexing

Much like Python's native lists and tuples, you can index and slice NumPy arrays.

a. Access individual elements using the square bracket notation:

```
import numpy as np


a = np.array([1, 2, 3, 4])

print(a[0])

print(a[2])
```

Output:

```
1

3
```

You could also use negative indices to access elements from the end of the array. For example:

```
import numpy as np
```

```
a = np.array([1, 2, 3, 4])

print(a[-1])

print(a[-2])
```

Output:

```
4

3
```

b. For slicing, employ the colon ':' operator:

```
import numpy as np

a = np.array([1, 2, 3, 4])

print(a[1:3])


b = np.array([[1, 2], [3, 4]])

print(b[:, 1])
```

Output:

```
[2, 3]

[2, 4]
```

You could use the colon : operator to indicate a step size. For example:

```
import numpy as np

```

```
a = np.array([1, 2, 3, 4])

print(a[::2])



b = np.array([[1, 2], [3, 4]])

print(b[::-1, ::-1])
```

Output:

```
[1, 3]

[[4, 3],[2, 1]]
```

Additionally, NumPy offers advanced indexing methods, including indexing via arrays of indices and boolean masks.

NumPy Array Operations

NumPy offers a variety of functions and operators for array operations. Standard arithmetic operators (+, -, *, etc.) enable element-wise operations. For instance:

```
import numpy as np

a = np.array([1, 2, 3, 4])

b = np.array([5, 6, 7, 8])



c = a + b  # element-wise addition

d = a - b  # element-wise subtraction

e = a * b  # element-wise multiplication

f = a / b  # element-wise division
```

NumPy's mathematical functions can be used for element-wise operations on arrays:

```
import numpy as np

a = np.array([1, 2, 3, 4])



b = np.sin(a)  # element-wise sine

c = np.cos(a)  # element-wise cosine

d = np.exp(a)  # element-wise exponential
```

We can also print any of the operation to see the output:

```
b = np.sin(a)

print(b)
```

Output:

```
[ 0.84147098  0.90929743  0.14112001 -0.7568025 ]
```

As you can see, the function sin() had performed sine operation on each element in the array.

NumPy also provides functions for performing aggregation (i.e., reducing) operations on arrays, for example sum, mean, and std (standard deviation):

```
a = np.array([[1, 2], [3, 4]])

b = np.sum(a)  # sum of all elements

c = np.sum(a, axis=0)  # sum of each column

d = np.sum(a, axis=1)  # sum of each row

e = np.mean(a)  # mean of all elements
```

```
f = np.mean(a, axis=0)  # mean of each column

g = np.mean(a, axis=1)  # mean of each row

h = np.std(a)  # standard deviation of all elements

i = np.std(a, axis=0)  # standard deviation of each column

j = np.std(a, axis=1)  # standard deviation of each row
```

NumPy also allows dot and cross product operations on arrays:

```
a = np.array([1, 2, 3])

b = np.array([4, 5, 6])

c = np.dot(a, b)  # dot product

d = np.cross(a, b)  # cross product
```

Again you can print the products to see the result of each operation.

Array Manipulation

There is a wide range of functions for manipulating arrays.

NumPy arrays can be reshaped provided the number of elements remain unchanged:

```
a = np.array([1, 2, 3, 4, 5, 6])

b = a.reshape((2, 3))  # reshape to (2, 3)

print(b)
```

Output:

```
[[1 2 3]

 [4 5 6]]
```

As you can see, we have changed the shape of the array

Transpose function flips the array along its diagonal:

```
a = np.array([[1, 2, 3], [4, 5, 6]])

b = a.transpose()

print(b.shape)
```

Output:

```
(3, 2)
```

The array passed from a shape of (2, 3) to a shape of (3, 2) because we have applied the transpose method.

Moreover, arrays can be flattened or concatenated.

a. The flatten function converts a multidimensional array into a 1-dimensional array:

```
a = np.array([[1, 2, 3], [4, 5, 6]])

b = a.flatten()  # flatten array



print(a.shape)

print(b.shape)
```

Output:

```
(2, 3)

(6, )
```

As you can see, after applying the flatten method, the array is just one-dimensional.

b. The concatenate function will concatenate arrays along a specific axis:

```
a = np.array([[1, 2], [3, 4]])
```

```
b = np.array([[5, 6], [7, 8]])


c = np.concatenate((a, b), axis=0)  # concatenate along rows

d = np.concatenate((a, b), axis=1)  # concatenate along columns


print(c)

print("\n")

print(d)
```

Output:

```
[[1 2]

[3 4]

[5 6]

[7 8]]


[[1 2 5 6]

[3 4 7 8]]
```

As you can see, we have performed a concatenation using rows and columns.

Linear algebra and statistics

NumPy offers a range of functions to execute linear algebra operations on arrays, including tasks like matrix multiplication, computing dot products, and determining matrix inverses.

a. To perform matrix multiplication on two arrays, you can use the dot function:

```
a = np.array([[1, 2], [3, 4]])

b = np.array([[5, 6], [7, 8]])


c = np.dot(a, b)  # matrix multiplication

print(c)
```

Output:

```
[[19 22] [43 50]]
```

b. To perform the dot product of two arrays, you can choose to apply the dot function or the @ operator:

```
import numpy as np

a = np.array([1, 2, 3])

b = np.array([4, 5, 6])


c = np.dot(a, b)  # dot product

d = a @ b  # dot product (alternative syntax)

print(c)

print(d)
```

Output:

```
32
```

c. To calculate the inverse of a matrix, there is the inv function:

```
a = np.array([[1, 2], [3, 4]])

b = np.linalg.inv(a)

print(b)
```

Output:

```
[[-2.   1. ] [ 1.5 -0.5]]
```

d. To calculate the determinant of a matrix, you can use the det function:

```
a = np.array([[1, 2], [3, 4]])

b = np.linalg.det(a)

print(b)
```

Output:

```
-2.0
```

e. To calculate the eigenvalues and eigenvectors of a matrix, you can use the eig function:

```
a = np.array([[1, 2], [3, 4]])

b, c = np.linalg.eig(a)  # eigenvalues and eigenvectors
```

```
print(b)

print(c)
```

Output:

```
[ -0.37228132  5.37228132]

[[-0.82456484 -0.41597356] [ 0.56576746 -0.90937671]]
```

f. To calculate the singular value decomposition of a matrix, you can use the svd function:

```
a = np.array([[1, 2], [3, 4]])

b, c, d = np.linalg.svd(a)  # singular value decomposition

print(b)

print(c)

print(d)
```

Output:

```
[ 5.4649857  0.82456484]

[[-0.       -0.82456484] [ 1.      0.56576746]]

[[-0.       -0.82456484] [ 1.      0.56576746]]
```

g. NumPy aids in calculating mean, median, and standard deviation:

```
a = np.array([1, 2, 3, 4, 5])
b = np.mean(a)
c = np.median(a)
d = np.std(a)
```

These functions can also operate along specified axes, by setting the axis parameter:

```
a = np.array([[1, 2, 3], [4, 5, 6]])

b = np.mean(a, axis=0)

c = np.median(a, axis=1)

d = np.std(a, axis=1)
```

NumPy array saving and reading

NumPy arrays can be saved as follows

```
a = np.array([1, 2, 3, 4, 5])

np.save('array.npy', a)
```

This will save the array in a separate file:

☐ 🗋 array.npy

To load an array from a file, you can use the load function:

```
a = np.load('array.npy')

print(a)
```

Output:

```
[1 2 3 4 5]
```

Chapter 16 - SciPy Module

SciPy is a Python-based library tailored for scientific computing, providing functions for array manipulation, numerical optimization, processing of signals and images, and conducting statistical analysis. SciPy builds upon the foundation set by the NumPy library, enhancing its capabilities with a vast range of algorithms and tools dedicated to scientific computations.

The structure of SciPy consists of several submodules, with each one tailored to a specific area of scientific computing. Some of the essential submodules include:

- **optimize**: Contains functions dedicated to optimizing objective functions, be it through minimization or maximization.
- **integrate**: Offers numerical integration tools, featuring algorithms suitable for both ordinary differential equations (ODEs) and partial differential equations (PDEs).
- **interpolate**: Houses functions for data interpolation, such as spline and polynomial interpolation methods.
- **signal**: Focuses on signal and image processing techniques.
- **sparse**: A module designed for handling sparse matrices.
- **linalg**: Encompasses linear algebra operations, boasting functionalities like matrix decomposition and computation of eigenvalues and eigenvectors.
- **stats**: Provides a myriad of statistical analysis functions and tools to handle probability distributions.

Here are some tips and best practices for optimal scipy use:

- Ensure NumPy is installed. Since scipy enhances the features of NumPy, having NumPy installed is essential to utilize scipy.
- Choose the appropriate data type. Since scipy functions predominantly work with NumPy arrays, selecting the correct data type for your data is crucial. If your dataset is large and primarily consists of zeros, consider using a sparse matrix. This approach can be memory-efficient and boost performance.

- Opt for in-place operations. A number of scipy functions offer in-place versions that alter an existing array instead of generating a new one. This method can be beneficial in terms of memory and can enhance performance, particularly with vast datasets.
- Prioritize vectorized operations. Both NumPy and scipy offer robust vectorized operations that are notably more efficient than looping. Aim to use these vectorized techniques over loops whenever feasible.

Installation and setup

To get started with SciPy, NumPy must be installed beforehand. Both libraries can be installed using **pip**, Python's package manager:

```
pip install numpy scipy
```

Another option is the Anaconda distribution, a popular choice for scientific computing in Python. To install via Anaconda:

```
conda install numpy scipy
```

After installation, incorporate them into your Python scripts or Jupyter notebooks with:

```
import numpy as np

import scipy as sp
```

Deep Dive into SciPy Submodules

SciPy is organized into a number of submodules, each of which provides functions and algorithms for a specific topic. Here are some of the key submodules in SciPy:

a. scipy.optimize

This submodule provides algorithms for optimizing (minimizing or maximizing) objective functions. It includes a variety of optimization algorithms such as linear programming, nonlinear optimization, and least squares optimization. Here are some of the key functions in the optimize submodule:

- **minimize**: Minimizes a given objective function.

- **curve_fit**: Fits a curve to a certain group of data points with a nonlinear least squares algorithm.

- **root**: Finds the roots of a function (points where the function is zero).

- **linprog**: Solves a linear programming problem.

In the following practical example, our goal is to use the minimize function to minimize the Rosenbrock function, which finds the minimum of the Rosenbrock function starting from the initial guess x0.

```python
from scipy.optimize import minimize

import numpy as np


def rosenbrock(x):
    return sum(100.0*(x[1:]-x[:-1]**2.0)**2.0 + (1-x[:-1])**2.0)


x0 = np.array([1.3, 0.7, 0.8, 1.9, 1.2])

res = minimize(rosenbrock, x0, method='nelder-mead')


print(res.x)
```

Output:

```
[0.99910115 0.99820923 0.99646346 0.99297555 0.98600385]
```

b. scipy.integrate

This submodule provides functions for numerical integration, including algorithms for integrating ordinary differential equations (ODEs), partial differential equations (PDEs), and functions of one or more variables.

Here are some of the key functions in the integrate submodule:

- **quad**: Numerically evaluates a definite integral.

- **fixed_quad**: Integrates a function with the fixed-sample Gaussian quadrature.

- **quadrature**: Integrates a function with the fixed-tolerance Gaussian quadrature.

- **romberg**: Integrates a function using Romberg integration.

- **odeint**: Solves a system of ordinary differential equations (ODEs).

Let's solve a simple ODE with the **odeint** function:

```python
from scipy.integrate import odeint


def func(y, t, a, b):

    return a*y**2 + b


y0 = 1

t = np.linspace(0, 1, 10)

a, b = 2, 3

sol = odeint(func, y0, t, args=(a, b))

print(sol)
```

Output:

```
[[1.00000000e+000]

[1.73782532e+000]

[3.44317148e+000]

[1.75734549e+001]

[2.60975738e+010]

[6.90524995e-310]

[6.90528876e-310]

[6.90528877e-310]

[6.90528884e-310]

[6.90528884e-310]]
```

The code has solved the ODE dy/dt = a*y**2 + b with initial condition y(0) = 1, at the points in the t array.

c. scipy.interpolate

This submodule provides interpolating tools, including algorithms for spline interpolation and polynomial interpolation. Interpolation is the process of estimating a function's value at a specific point based on its values at adjacent points.

Here are some of the key functions in the interpolate submodule:

- **interp1d**: Interpolates a 1-dimensional function.

- **interp2d**: Interpolates a 2-dimensional function.

- **splrep**: Computes the spline representation of a curve.

- **splev**: Evaluates a spline or its derivatives.

In the following example, our goal is to interpolate 1-dimensional function [y = cos(x)] at 50 equally spaced points between 0 and 10.

```
from scipy.interpolate import interp1d

x = np.linspace(0, 10, 10)

y = np.cos(x)


f = interp1d(x, y)

xnew = np.linspace(0, 10, 50)

ynew = f(xnew)
```

d. scipy.signal

It provides functions for signal and image processing. Some of the key functions include:

- **convolve**: Convolves two N-dimensional arrays.

- **correlate**: Cross-correlates two N-dimensional arrays.

- **fftconvolve**: Convolves two N-dimensional arrays with the fast Fourier transform (FFT).

- **convolve2d**: Convolves a 2-dimensional array with a kernel.

- **medfilt**: Applies a median filter to a 1- or 2-dimensional array.

- **wiener**: Performs a Wiener filter on an N-dimensional array.

Let's see how to convolve two 1-dimensional arrays with the **convolve** function:

```
from scipy.signal import convolve
```

```
x = np.array([1, 2, 3])

y = np.array([0, 1, 0.5])


z = convolve(x, y)


print(z)
```

Output:

```
[0.  1.  2.5 4.  1.5]
```

The code has convolved the arrays x and y, resulting in the array [0, 1, 2.5, 4, 1.5].

e. scipy.sparse

This module provides functions for creating, manipulating, and solving systems of equations using sparse matrices. These matrices are characterized by a significant number of zero elements, and are often used in scientific and engineering applications to represent large, sparse systems of equations. Here are some of the key functions in the sparse submodule:

- **csr_matrix**: Builds a sparse matrix using the Compressed Sparse Row (CSR) format.

- **csc_matrix**: Creates a sparse matrix in the Compressed Sparse Column (CSC) format.

- **linalg.spsolve**: Solves a linear system of equations using sparse matrices.

- **linalg.eigs**: Computes the eigenvalues and eigenvectors of a sparse matrix.

In the following example we want to create a sparse matrix:

```
from scipy.sparse import csr_matrix
```

```
data = [1, 2, 3, 4]

indices = [0, 2, 2, 1]

indptr = [0, 2, 3, 4]


A = csr_matrix((data, indices, indptr), shape=(3, 3))

print(A)
```

Output:

```
(0, 0)   1

 (0, 2)  2

 (1, 2)  3

 (2, 1)  4
```

f. scipy.linalg

It offers a suite of functions for linear algebra tasks, including solving linear equation systems, performing matrix decompositions, and calculating eigenvalues and eigenvectors. Notable functions in the linalg submodule include:

- **solve**: Resolves the linear equation system Ax = b

- **inv**: Determines the inverse of a given matrix.

- **qr**: Calculates the QR decomposition for a matrix.

- **svd**: Computes the singular value decomposition (SVD) of a matrix.

- **eig**: Computes the eigenvalues and eigenvectors of a matrix.

Let's see how to solve a system of linear equations:

```
from scipy.linalg import solve


A = np.array([[1, 2], [3, 4]])

b = np.array([1, 2])

x = solve(A, b)

print(x)
```

Output:

```
[0. 0.5]
```

g. Scipy.stats

It provides functions for statistical analysis and probability distributions. It includes functions for estimating statistical parameters, testing hypotheses, and generating random variables from various probability distributions. Here are some of the key functions in the stats submodule:

- **norm.fit**: Estimates the parameters of a normal distribution from data.

- **t.fit**: Estimates the parameters of a t-distribution from data.

- **ttest_ind**: Computes the t-test for the means of two independent samples.

- **linregress**: Computes a linear regression on data.

- **chisquare**: Tests the goodness of fit of an observed distribution to a theoretical one.

- **rvs**: Generates random variables from a given probability distribution.

Now we want to estimate the parameters of a normal distribution with the norm.fit function:

```
from scipy.stats import norm


data = [0.5, 0.7, 1.0, 1.2, 1.3, 2.1]

mu, std = norm.fit(data)

print(mu, std)
```

Output:

```
1.1333333333333335 0.5120763831912405
```

The code calculated the mean and standard deviation of the best-fitting normal distribution for the data.

Chapter 17 - Matplotlib Module

Matplotlib facilitates the creation of a myriad of static, animated, and interactive visualizations. It stands as a multifaceted Python library for data visualization, enabling the creation of diverse visual displays like line plots, scatter plots, bar plots, error bars, histograms, pie charts, and box plots, among others.

Line Plots in Matplotlib

A line plot visualizes data on a number line and typically depicts the distribution of a continuous variable. To generate a line plot in Matplotlib, employ the **plot** function:

```python
import matplotlib.pyplot as plt


# Sample data

x = [1, 2, 3, 4, 5]

y = [2, 3, 7, 1, 4]


# Generate the plot

plt.plot(x, y)


# Display the plot

plt.show()
```

Output:

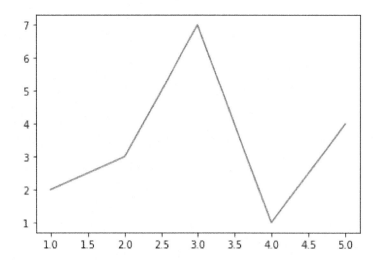

Matplotlib allows for extensive customization of visuals. For instance, in a line plot, you can modify the line color and style through the 'color' and 'linestyle' parameters. Enhancements like axis labels and titles can be added using the 'xlabel', 'ylabel', and 'title' functions.

Here is an example with a red dashed line plot complemented by axis labels and a title.

```python
# Generate the plot

plt.plot(x, y, color='red', linestyle='dashed')


# Add axis labels and a title

plt.xlabel('Position')

plt.ylabel('Value')

plt.title('Line Plot Example')


# Display the plot

plt.show()
```

Output:

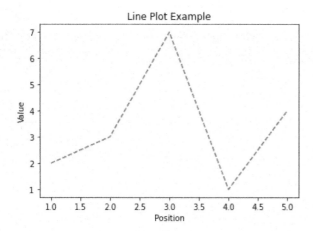

Scatter plots in Matplotlib

Scatter plots showcase data points on horizontal and vertical axes to illustrate the relationship between two continuous variables. In matplotlib, you can generate a scatter plot using the **scatter** function:

```
# Generate the plot

plt.scatter(x, y)

# Display the plot

plt.show()
```

Output:

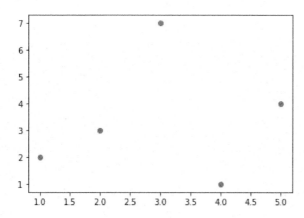

Customizations, such as altering the marker color and size, can be done with the **color** and **s** parameters, respectively. You could add axis labels and a title with the **xlabel, ylabel,** and **title** functions. The following is a demonstration of a scatter plot featuring red markers, each 100 points in size, accompanied by axis labels and a title.

```
# Generate the plot

plt.scatter(x, y, color='red', s=100)


# Add axis labels and a title

plt.xlabel('Position')

plt.ylabel('Value')

plt.title('Scatter Plot Example')


# Display the plot

plt.show()
```

Output:

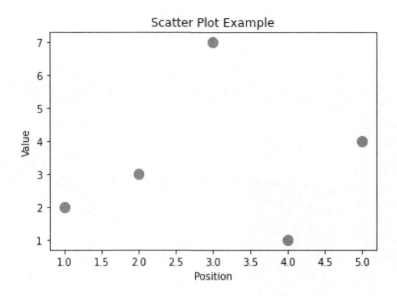

Bar plots in Matplotlib module

Bar plots present data through bars, highlighting the distribution of a categorical variable. You will use the **bar** function:

```
import matplotlib.pyplot as plt


# Sample data

x = ['Group 1', 'Group 2', 'Group 3']

y = [3, 6, 4]


# Generate the plot

plt.bar(x, y)


# Display the plot
```

```
plt.show()
```

Output:

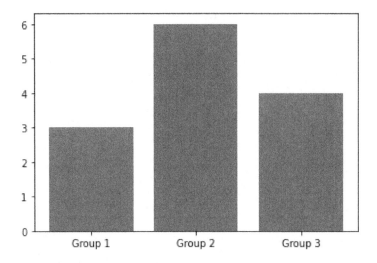

As we did for previous plots, here is an example of a more customized bar plot:

```
# Generate the plot

plt.bar(x, y, color='red')


# Add axis labels and a title

plt.xlabel('Group')

plt.ylabel('Value')

plt.title('Bar Plot Example')


# Display the plot

plt.show()
```

Output:

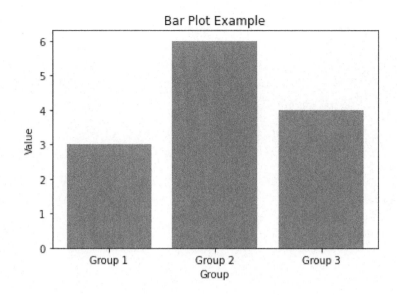

There are different types of bar plots that you can create in matplotlib. For example, you can opt for a horizontal bar plot and in this case you will use the **barh** function instead of the **bar** function. Let' see an example:

```
# Generate the plot

plt.barh(x, y)



# Display the plot

plt.show()
```

Output:

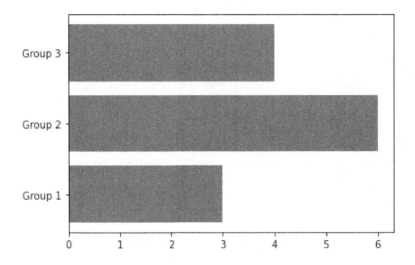

Moreover, a stacked bar plot can be generated with the **bar** function coupled with the **bottom** argument.

A stacked bar chart compartmentalizes bars into segments, each symbolizing a distinct category. Let's see an example illustrating horizontal and stacked bar plots. In the following example the goal is to generate a stacked bar plot with red bars representing y1 values and blue bars representing y2 values. The bottom argument specifies the starting position of the bars on the vertical axis.

```
# Generate the plot

plt.bar(x, y1, color='red')

plt.bar(x, y2, color='blue', bottom=y1)



# Display the plot

plt.show()
```

Ouptut:

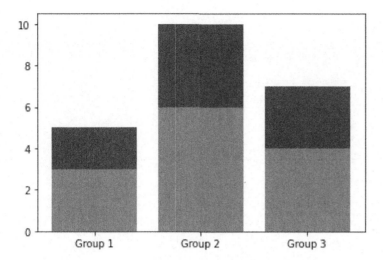

Histogram plots in Matplotlib

Histograms graphically represent data distribution of a continuous variable by indicating the frequency of various value ranges. Data is segmented into bins, with each bin's height reflecting the number of data points it encompasses. These bins, typically of uniform size, are juxtaposed to construct the histogram.

It's essential to understand which is the difference between bar charts and histograms is essential: bar charts compare different categories, whereas histograms showcase a continuous variable's distribution.

Here's how to generate a histogram:

```
import matplotlib.pyplot as plt


# Sample data

data = [1, 2, 2, 3, 3, 3, 4, 4, 4, 4, 5, 5, 5, 5, 5]
```

```
# Create the histogram

plt.hist(data)



# Display the plot

plt.show()
```

Output:

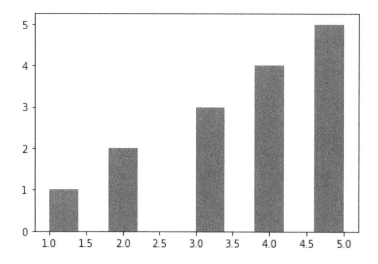

Customization, such as adjusting the bin count or the plotted value range, can be done using **bins** and **range** parameters, respectively. As always, with **xlabel**, **ylabel**, and **title** we can add axis labels and titles:

```
# Create the histogram

plt.hist(data, bins=8, range=(0, 6))



# Add axis labels and a title

plt.xlabel('Value')
```

```
plt.ylabel('Frequency')

plt.title('Histogram Example')


# Display the plot

plt.show()
```

Output:

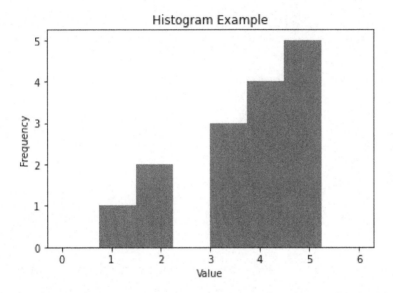

Matplotlib also offers variations of histograms, like stacked histograms using the **stacked** parameter or normalized histograms via the **density** argument. Here's a representation of a stacked histogram.

```
# creating  the data

data1 = [1, 2, 2, 3, 3, 3, 4, 4, 4, 4, 5, 5, 5, 5, 5]

data2 = [0, 1, 1, 2, 2, 2, 3, 3, 3, 3, 4, 4, 4, 4, 4]
```

```
# creating histogram

plt.hist([data1, data2], stacked=True)



plt.show()
```

Output:

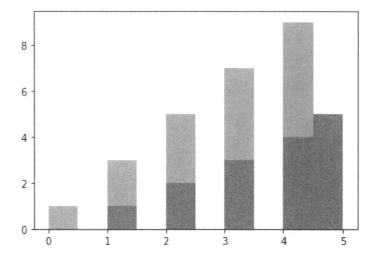

Pie charts in matplotlib

A pie chart displays data as a circular graph segmented into slices, each symbolizing a portion of the whole. The length of each slice's arc in the pie chart directly corresponds to the value it denotes. In matplotlib, the function to be used when you want to generate a pie chart is the **pie** function:

```
import matplotlib.pyplot as plt



# Sample data

sizes = [15, 30, 45, 10]

labels = ['Group 1', 'Group 2', 'Group 3', 'Group 4']
```

```
# Create the pie chart

plt.pie(sizes, labels=labels)

# Display the plot

plt.show()
```

Output:

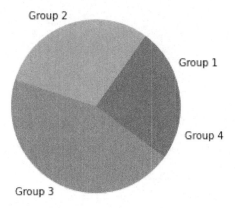

The appearance of the pie chart is customizable. For instance, slice colors can be modified using the **colors** argument, while the starting angle of the initial slice can be adjusted with the **startangle** argument. Titles can be incorporated using the **title** function. Let's create a more customized pie chart:

```
# Sample data

sizes = [15, 30, 45, 10]

labels = ['Group 1', 'Group 2', 'Group 3', 'Group 4']

colors = ['red', 'green', 'blue', 'yellow']


# Create the pie chart
```

```
plt.pie(sizes, labels=labels, colors=colors, startangle=90)


# Add a title

plt.title('Pie Chart Example')


# Display the plot

plt.show()
```

We can create different types of pie charts: for example, a donut chart can be generated by employing the **pie** function with the **wedgeprops** argument, or an exploded pie chart can be designed using the **explode** argument. Let's see a pie chart with exploded slices:

```
# Sample data

sizes = [15, 30, 45, 10]

labels = ['Group 1', 'Group 2', 'Group 3', 'Group 4']

explode = (0, 0.1, 0, 0)


# Create the pie chart

plt.pie(sizes, labels=labels, explode=explode)


# Display the plot

plt.show()
```

Output:

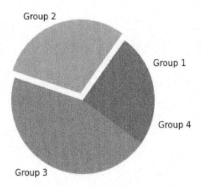

Box plots in Matplotlib

Also referred to as a whisker plot, a box plot graphically delineates data, indicating its minimum, first quartile, median, third quartile, and maximum; it is invaluable for grasping data distribution and spotting outliers. With Matplotlib's **boxplot** function, creating a box plot becomes straightforward. Let's see an example:

```
# Sample data

data = [1, 2, 2, 3, 3, 3, 4, 4, 4, 4, 5, 5, 5, 5, 5]


# Create the box plot

plt.boxplot(data)


# Display the plot

plt.show()
```

Output:

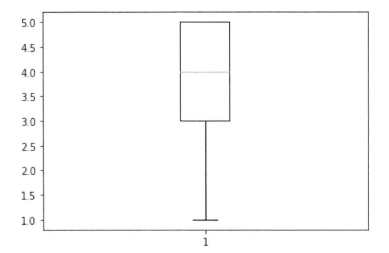

As you can see the code has created a box plot with the data points 1, 2, 2, 3, 3, 3, 4, 4, 4, 4, 5, 5, 5, 5, 5. The box in the plot is a visual representation of the interquartile range (which is the middle 50% of the total data), the central line inside this box indicates the median, while the whiskers represent the lower and upper quartiles (25% and 75% of the data). Data points outside the whisker's span are considered outliers.

Heatmaps in Matplotlib
A heatmap conveys data through color variations, and it is useful to identify and visualize patterns and trends in defined sets of data. You can generate a heatmap using the **imshow** function:

```
import matplotlib.pyplot as plt

import numpy as np


# Sample data

data = np.array([[1, 2, 3, 4], [5, 6, 7, 8], [9, 10, 11, 12]])
```

```
# Create the heatmap

plt.imshow(data, cmap='YlGnBu')



# Add a colorbar

plt.colorbar()



# Display the plot

plt.show()
```

Output:

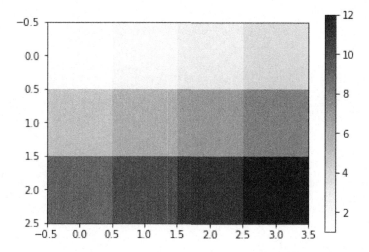

The resulting heatmap encompasses three rows and four columns, with values depicted in color shades from the 'hot' colormap. The **interpolation** argument specifies how the values are interpolated to determine the color at each pixel.

Contour plots
These plots render a 3D dataset visually, with the z-axis value denoted by the color intensity of points; they are used to visualize patterns in data, and for identifying trends and correlations. In this case we'll use the **contour** function:

```
import matplotlib.pyplot as plt

import numpy as np


# Sample data

X = np.linspace(-5, 5, 100)

Y = np.linspace(-5, 5, 100)

X, Y = np.meshgrid(X, Y)

Z = np.sin(X**2 + Y**2)


# Create the contour plot

plt.contour(X, Y, Z, colors='k')


# Display the plot

plt.show()
```

Output:

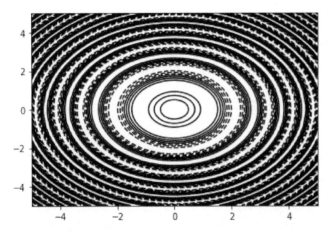

As always, you can also reach a higher level of customization changing the colors of the contours using the **colors** argument, or adding a colorbar using the **colorbar** function. An example of a more customized contour plot could be the following:

```
# Sample data

X = np.linspace(-5, 5, 100)

Y = np.linspace(-5, 5, 100)

X, Y = np.meshgrid(X, Y)

Z = np.sin(X**2 + Y**2)


# Create the contour plot

plt.contour(X, Y, Z, colors='k')


# Add a colorbar

plt.colorbar()


# Display the plot

plt.show()
```

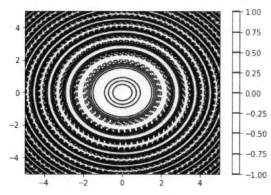

In Matplotlib, one can experiment with various contour plot styles; you can obtain a filled contour plot with the **contourf** function, and a 3D representation is attainable using the **plot_surface** function. Let's see an example of a filled contour plot:

```
# Sample data

X = np.linspace(-5, 5, 100)

Y = np.linspace(-5, 5, 100)

X, Y = np.meshgrid(X, Y)

Z = np.sin(X**2 + Y**2)


# Create the contour plot

plt.contourf(X, Y, Z, cmap='viridis')

# Display the plot

plt.show()
```

Output:

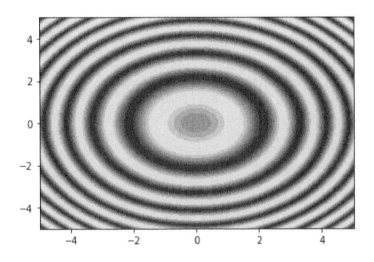

Chapter 18 - Keras Module

Keras is a robust and easy to understand library for deep learning. It offers an array of model architectures and pre-trained models, making it an excellent starting point for custom model development. Furthermore, it provides tools for designing and adapting models from the ground up.

To begin with Keras, installation is required, along with a backend engine like TensorFlow. Once set up, Keras empowers users to design and educate deep learning models utilizing the Sequential Model or the more flexible Functional Model API.

The Sequential model facilitates a consecutive stack of layers, enabling users to add layers sequentially. In contrast, the Functional Model API caters to the development of intricate models by denoting layers and their interconnections functionally.

Once a model is constructed, it's compiled by selecting the loss function, optimizer, and any additional metrics for monitoring. The **fit** method then trains the model on data. Model performance on specific datasets can be gauged using the **evaluate** method, and predictions on new data are made using the **predict** method. Additionally, Keras provides the flexibility of using pre-trained models as foundations or tweaking existing models by layer adjustments.

Before installing Keras, ensure TensorFlow or Theano is on your system. If not, TensorFlow can be installed via the TensorFlow website and Theano via its official website. With either TensorFlow or Theano in place, Keras can be installed using any of the following commands:

- if you are using pip >> pip install keras
- if you are using pip3 version >> pip3 install keras
- if you are using anaconda >> conda install keras
- if you are using jupyter-notebook >> !pip install keras

Building a Neural network in Keras

The first step when you want to build a neural network with Keras is to define the model:

a. Sequential model

To define a Sequential model, all you need to do is generate a new Sequential object and start adding layers to it using the **add** method. Let's see the code to generate a simple Sequential model with a single fully-connected (Dense) layer with 10 units:

```
from keras.models import Sequential

from keras.layers import Dense


model = Sequential()

model.add(Dense(units=10, input_shape=(64,)))
```

Here, the **units** parameter indicates the layer's unit count, while **input_shape** designates the input data shape. In our example, a data with 64 features has an input shape of (64,). You can add additional layers to the model using the **add** function again with a new layer. For example, the following code adds another fully-connected layer with 5 units:

```
model.add(Dense(units=5))
```

b. Functional Model:

Defining a model using the Functional Model API requires initializing an Input layer, defining the input data shape, and then creating subsequent layers linked to this input. The following code creates a simple model with a single fully-connected (Dense) layer with 10 units:

```
from keras.layers import Input, Dense

from keras.models import Model
```

```
inputs = Input(shape=(64,))

x = Dense(units=10)(inputs)

model = Model(inputs=inputs, outputs=x)
```

Compiling and training model

Once you've constructed your model, the subsequent phase is compiling it. In Keras, compiling involves defining the loss function, optimizer, and potentially additional metrics for monitoring throughout training.

For the compile process in Keras, employ the compile method with key parameters like:

- **loss**: Defines the loss function the model aims to minimize. Typical choices include mean squared error (MSE) for regression tasks and categorical crossentropy for classification tasks.
- **optimizer**: This is the algorithm employed by the model to optimize weight selection. Standard optimizers are stochastic gradient descent (SGD), Adam, and RMSprop.
- **metrics**: An optional list of additional performance measures to monitor during training, such as accuracy in classification tasks

Here's an illustrative snippet for compiling a model in Keras.

```
model.compile(loss='categorical_crossentropy',

        optimizer='sgd',

        metrics=['accuracy'])
```

Once compiled, progress to training your model using the **fit** method. Essential parameters include:

- x: Represents the input data, typically as a Numpy array shaped (n_samples, n_features) for single-input models, or a list of arrays for models with multiple inputs.

- y: Denotes the target data, usually a Numpy array shaped (n_samples, n_classes) for single-output models, or a list of arrays for multiple outputs.
- batch_size: Determines the sample size for each update during training.
- epochs: Specifies the total number of passes through the entire dataset.
- validation_data: Optionally, a tuple (x_val, y_val) for validation.

Below is an example demonstrating how to train a Keras model.

```
history = model.fit(x_train, y_train,

        batch_size=32, epochs=10,

        validation_data=(x_val, y_val))
```

During training, the model iteratively adjusts its weights based on the specified loss function and optimizer. It evaluates the validation data (if provided) at each epoch's end and computes any defined metrics.

You can retrieve training statistics from the **history** attribute of the returned History object. It's a dictionary with epoch-wise training and validation loss and metrics, useful for visualizing training trends and spotting overfitting or underfitting.

Finally, apply the **predict** method for generating predictions on new data, which requires a Numpy array of input data and yields a corresponding array of predictions.

```
predictions = model.predict(x_test)
```

Now, our model has predicted the output values using the testing data which only contain the input values.

Evaluating Model Performance

Once your model is trained, it's crucial to assess its performance on data it hasn't seen before. This evaluation helps determine how well the model generalizes to new data and whether it's prone to overfitting or underfitting. For this purpose, the **evaluate** method is employed, requiring specific parameters:

- x: Refers to the input data, which should be a Numpy array with a shape of (n_samples, n_features) for models with a single input. For models with multiple inputs, a list of Numpy arrays is required.
- y: Represents the target data. For models with a single output, this should be a Numpy array shaped (n_samples, n_classes). For multiple outputs, a list of Numpy arrays is necessary.
- batch_size: An optional parameter specifying the number of samples in each batch. If omitted, the method processes the whole dataset.
- verbose: Another optional parameter that, when enabled, displays progress updates.

The **evaluate** method produces a list of metric values based on the loss function and metrics defined during the model's compilation stage. For instance, if the model was compiled with categorical crossentropy loss and an accuracy metric, **evaluate** will return both the loss and accuracy figures for the provided data.

```
loss, accuracy = model.evaluate(x_test, y_test)

print('Test loss:', loss)

print('Test accuracy:', accuracy)
```

In addition to **evaluate**, the **predict** method is available for generating predictions on new datasets. Subsequently, you can calculate performance metrics using external functions. For instance, in classification models, the **accuracy_score** function from **sklearn.metrics** can be utilized to determine the accuracy of these predictions.

```
from sklearn.metrics import accuracy_score

predictions = model.predict(x_test)

accuracy = accuracy_score(y_test, predictions)

print('Test accuracy:', accuracy)
```

This will print the accuracy of the model.

Saving and loading the model

Keras allows you to save models for future use or sharing. The **save** method stores the model architecture, weights, and optimizer state in an HDF5 file:

```
model.save('model.h5')
```

You can then load the model from this file using the **load_model** function:

```
from keras.models import load_model

model = load_model('model.h5')
```

The save method also accepts several optional arguments, such as **save_format** to specify the file format to use, and **include_optimizer** to specify whether to include the optimizer state in the saved file.

The **save_weights** method can be used to save the weights of a model to a separate file:

```
model.save_weights('weights.h5')
```

And with the **load_weights** method you could load the weights into a model:

```
model.load_weights('weights.h5')
```

Remember that the model architecture must be the same when you load the weights, otherwise the load will fail. In case your goal is to load weights into a different model architecture, you will need first to create the new model with the desired architecture, and then load the weights into the new model.

Using pre-trained models

Using pre-trained models is a convenient way to leverage the knowledge gained from large-scale training on a specific task and apply it to a new task. In Keras, you can use the Applications module to load a pre-trained model and use it as a starting point for your own model.

For example, to use the VGG19 model pre-trained on the ImageNet dataset, follow this code:

```
from keras.applications import VGG19

model = VGG19(weights='imagenet')
```

This will download the VGG19 model and its weights from the Internet and create a new model with the weights initialized from the pre-trained model. You can then use this model as a starting point for your own model by adding additional layers and compiling and training it.

```
x = model.output

x = Dense(1024, activation='relu')(x)

predictions = Dense(10, activation='softmax')(x)


model = Model(inputs=model.input, outputs=predictions)

model.compile(loss='categorical_crossentropy',

        optimizer='sgd',

        metrics=['accuracy'])


model.fit(x_train, y_train, epochs=5, batch_size=32)
```

You can also specify which layers of the pre-trained model to fine-tune by setting the trainable attribute of the layer to True:

```
for layer in model.layers[:-4]:

   layer.trainable = False
```

```
model.compile(loss='categorical_crossentropy',

        optimizer='sgd',

        metrics=['accuracy'])



model.fit(x_train, y_train, epochs=5, batch_size=32)
```

This will freeze the weights of the first few layers of the pre-trained model, so that they are not updated during training. This can be useful when using a pre-trained model as a feature extractor, or when you want to fine-tune only a few layers of the model.

In the Applications module you will find several pre-trained models, including models for image classification, object detection, and more. A list of available models is available in the official documentation at the following link: https://keras.io/api/applications.

Customizing models

In addition to using pre-trained models, you can also customize models in Keras by adding or modifying layers. This can be useful in case your goals is to create a model that is tailored to a specific task, or when you want to experiment with different architectures to identify the best solution for your specific problem. To customize a model in Keras, you will need to use the functional Model API, which allows you to specify the layers and how they are connected as functions. Let's see how to build a simple fully-connected model with the functional Model API:

```
from keras.layers import Input, Dense

from keras.models import Model



inputs = Input(shape=(64,))
```

```
x = Dense(units=64, activation='relu')(inputs)

x = Dense(units=64, activation='relu')(x)

predictions = Dense(units=10, activation='softmax')(x)



model = Model(inputs=inputs, outputs=predictions)
```

This creates a model with two hidden layers and an output layer. You can then compile and train your model with the compile and fit methods, as usual.

```
model.compile(loss='categorical_crossentropy',

        optimizer='sgd',

        metrics=['accuracy'])


model.fit(x_train, y_train, epochs=5, batch_size=32)
```

The functional Model API can be utilized to construct more intricate models, including those with multiple inputs or outputs, as well as models that incorporate shared layers. For example, to create a model with two inputs and one output, you can do the following:

```
from keras.layers import Input, Dense

from keras.models import Model



input_a = Input(shape=(64,))

input_b = Input(shape=(128,))
```

```
x = Dense(units=64)(input_a)

y = Dense(units=64)(input_b)

z = keras.layers.concatenate([x, y])

predictions = Dense(units=10, activation='softmax')(z)


model = Model(inputs=[input_a, input_b], outputs=predictions)
```

This creates a model with two input layers and a single output layer. You can then compile and train your model with the compile and fit methods, as usual.

```
model.compile(loss='categorical_crossentropy',

        optimizer='sgd',

        metrics=['accuracy'])


model.fit([x_train_a, x_train_b], y_train, epochs=5, batch_size=32)
```

Customizing models in Keras is a powerful way to build models tailored to your specific needs. However, it can be more complex than using the Sequential model or pre-trained models, especially for beginners.

Chapter 19 - Sklearn module

Scikit-learn, often referred to as sklearn, is a widely used Python library dedicated to machine learning. It encompasses a variety of tools and functions to facilitate tasks such as classification, regression, clustering, dimensionality reduction, model selection, and preprocessing.

Key features of scikit-learn include:

- Powerful tools tailored for data analysis and mining.
- A comprehensive collection of machine learning algorithms, spanning both supervised and unsupervised learning.
- A uniform interface across different machine learning models, enabling easy transitions between them.
- A suite of utilities to aid in model assessment, including functionalities like train-test splits, cross-validation, and diverse performance metrics.
- Integration with core scientific libraries like NumPy, SciPy, and matplotlib.

Installation and setup

The most common way to install the module is with **pip**, the Python package manager. Open a terminal and type:

```
pip install scikit-learn
```

Alternatively, you can install scikit-learn using conda, the package manager for Anaconda:

```
conda install -c anaconda scikit-learn
```

Once you have installed scikit-learn, you can import it in your Python code writing the following statement:

```
import sklearn
```

Data Preprocessing

Data preprocessing is a fundamental step in machine learning. It pertains to the refinement and setup of data prior to analysis, laying a foundation for effective model creation. Scikit-learn offers an assortment of classes and functions to streamline data preprocessing.

Prior to implementing machine learning algorithms on a dataset, it is crucial to undergo data preprocessing. This process encompasses several key stages, such as:

- Ingesting the data.
- Addressing missing data.
- Transforming categorical variables.
- Dividing the data into training and testing segments.

Below is an example of how to import a dataset and divide it into training and test sets utilizing scikit-learn:

```
from sklearn.datasets import load_iris

from sklearn.model_selection import train_test_split


# Load the iris dataset

X, y = load_iris(return_X_y=True)


# Split the data into training and test sets

X_train, X_test, y_train, y_test = train_test_split(X, y, test_size=0.3, random_state=42)
```

Here, **load_iris** retrieves the built-in iris datase, which is included with scikit-learn. The **train_test_split** function in scikit-learn divides data into training and test sets. The **test_size** parameter designates the portion of data to allocate to the test set. For instance, if **test_size** is set to 0.3, it means 30% of the data will constitute the test set. The **random_state** parameter determines the seed for the random number generator, ensuring that data shuffling prior to the split remains consistent.

To handle missing values, you can use the **SimpleImputer** class from scikit-learn. The **fit_transform** method, when used with data imputers in scikit-learn, adjusts the imputer according to the training data and then outputs the imputed data. Conversely, the **transform** method applies the previously determined imputation process to the test data.

Here is an example:

```python
from sklearn.impute import SimpleImputer


# Create an instance of the SimpleImputer class

imputer = SimpleImputer(strategy='mean')


# Impute the missing values in the training data

X_train_imputed = imputer.fit_transform(X_train)


# Impute the missing values in the test data

X_test_imputed = imputer.transform(X_test)
```

For handling categorical variables in your dataset, scikit-learn offers the **OneHotEncoder** class:

```python
from sklearn.preprocessing import OneHotEncoder

# Create an instance of the OneHotEncoder class
```

```
encoder = OneHotEncoder()


# Encode the categorical variables in the training data

X_train_encoded = encoder.fit_transform(X_train_imputed)


# Encode the categorical variables in the test data

X_test_encoded = encoder.transform(X_test_imputed)
```

When applied, the **fit_transform** method tunes the encoder using the training data and subsequently returns data that's been one-hot encoded. On the other hand, the **transform** method takes the earlier configured encoding scheme and applies it to the test data.

The final step in preparing your data for machine learning involves segmenting it into distinct sets: typically training, validation, and test sets. This division is essential as it allows you to gauge how well your model will likely perform on data it hasn't seen during the training phase, aiding in the mitigation of overfitting.

Within scikit-learn, the **train_test_split** function is a handy tool for this purpose:

```
from sklearn.model_selection import train_test_split

X_train, X_test, y_train, y_test = train_test_split(X, y, test_size=0.2, random_state=42)
```

Assuming **X** and **y** represent the input features and target outcomes respectively, the **test_size** parameter is used to define what fraction of the entire dataset should be designated as the test set. Meanwhile, the **random_state** parameter ensures consistency in data shuffling across different runs by setting a specific seed for the random number generator.

Regression algorithms

Regression algorithms predict continuous values, such as stock prices or weather temperatures. Some prominent regression algorithms within the scikit-learn (often referred to as **sklearn**) library include:

- **Linear Regression**: A straightforward technique assuming a linear relationship between predictor and response variables. Use the **LinearRegression** class for implementation.

- **Polynomial Regression**: Represents the relationship between predictors and response as an n-th degree polynomial. Combine the **PolynomialFeatures** class for data transformation and **LinearRegression** class for model fitting.

- **Ridge Regression**: A regularized version of linear regression, adding a penalty to deter overfitting. Utilize the **Ridge** class for its application.

- **Lasso Regression**: Another regularized form of linear regression, but with an L1 penalty which can nullify certain coefficients. The **Lasso** class enables its implementation.

Let's see linear regression with an example:

```
from sklearn.linear_model import LinearRegression


# Create an instance of the LinearRegression class

model = LinearRegression()


# Fit the model to the training data

model.fit(X_train, y_train)

# Make predictions on the test data

y_pred = model.predict(X_test)
```

In similar way, you can import other regression algorithms, train the models and make predictions.

Classification algorithms

Classification algorithms predict categorical class labels, finding utility in applications like email filtering and facial recognition. Notable classifiers in scikit-learn encompass:

- **Logistic Regression**: A method estimating the probability of class membership via a logistic function. Implemented using the **LogisticRegression** class.

- **Decision Trees**: Tree-based models deciding based on predictor values. They're interpretable but might overfit. Use the **DecisionTreeClassifier** class for decision trees.

- **Random Forests**: An ensemble method aggregating multiple decision tree predictions. Less overfit-prone, but potentially computation-intensive. The **RandomForestClassifier** class facilitates its application.

- **Support Vector Machines (SVMs)**: Aim to identify the optimal hyperplane separating classes, suitable for high-dimensional data. The **SVC** class in scikit-learn can be used.

- **Naive Bayes**: A probabilistic classifier leveraging Bayes' theorem for predictions.

- **K-Nearest Neighbors (KNN)**: A non-parametric method classifying based on the majority class among K closest neighbors.

Let's use the logistic regression in practice:

```
from sklearn.linear_model import LogisticRegression


# Create an instance of the LogisticRegression class

model = LogisticRegression()
```

```
# Fit the model to the training data

model.fit(X_train, y_train)



# Make predictions on the test data

y_pred = model.predict(X_test)
```

As you can see, first, we have imported the algorithms, then we have trained the model by fitting training data and then we have made predictions using testing data.

Clustering algorithms

Clustering algorithms serve the purpose of grouping data points with similar characteristics. These algorithms find widespread applications in areas such as market segmentation, image categorization, and anomaly identification.

Within the scikit-learn framework, these algorithms fall under the umbrella of clustering models. Here are some of the notable clustering models available in scikit-learn:

- **K-means clustering:** This centroid-based method seeks to divide data into 'K' distinct clusters. The primary objective is to minimize the cumulative distance between data points and the centroid of their respective clusters. For implementing K-means clustering in scikit-learn, the **KMeans** class is your go-to tool.

- **Hierarchical clustering:** This method constructs a tree-like hierarchy of clusters. Broadly speaking, we can identify 2 kinds of hierarchical clustering: agglomerative and divisive. Scikit-learn offers the **AgglomerativeClustering** class for the agglomerative type, while the divisive type is typically achieved using methods like DBSCAN.

- **DBSCAN (Density-Based Spatial Clustering of Applications with Noise):** As a density-centric method, DBSCAN identifies and groups densely populated data points, while categorizing sparser points as noise. This approach is particularly resilient to outliers and does away with the need to clarify the exact quantity of clusters beforehand. The **DBSCAN** class in scikit-learn facilitates the use of this algorithm.

Let's see K-means clustering in practice:

```
from sklearn.cluster import KMeans


# Create an instance of the KMeans class

model = KMeans(n_clusters=3)


# Fit the model to the data

model.fit(X)

# Predict the cluster labels for the data

y_pred = model.predict(X)
```

Model Evaluation and Selection

Evaluating and selecting models is a fundamental phase in the machine learning pipeline. This process entails assessing multiple machine learning models to identify which one excels based on specified criteria. The significance of this step cannot be understated, given that a model's performance directly influences the accuracy of its predictions.

The scikit-learn library comes with a variety of utilities and methodologies to aid in model evaluation and selection. Here are a few notable ones:

- **Cross-validation:** This is a resampling strategy where the dataset is partitioned into several "folds". For each fold iteration, the model undergoes training on a subset and is subsequently evaluated on the remaining data. This method offers an effective means to gauge the model's generalization capabilities and facilitates comparisons between different models. The **cross_val_score** function allows for the implementation of cross-validation.

- **Grid search:** Hyperparameter tuning is integral to refining model performance. The grid search technique aids this by exploring a predefined grid of hyperparameters, training models for every unique combination, and eventually settling on the one that manifests the best performance metrics. The **GridSearchCV** class in scikit-learn is designed for this specific purpose.

- **Metrics:** To quantify the performance of machine learning models, scikit-learn encompasses a variety of metrics. For tasks centered around classification, metrics like accuracy, precision, and recall can be employed. On the other hand, for regression-centric tasks, measures like the mean absolute error and the root mean squared error are often utilized.

How to use **cross-validation** to evaluate a model in scikit-learn:

```
from sklearn.model_selection import cross_val_score



# Evaluate the model using 5-fold cross-validation

scores = cross_val_score(model, X, y, cv=5)
```

Now we want to apply the **grid search** to identify the best hyperparameters for a model:

```
from sklearn.model_selection import GridSearchCV



# Define the hyperparameter grid

param_grid = {'n_estimators': [10, 20, 30],

        'max_depth': [None, 10, 20]}
```

```
# Create an instance of the GridSearchCV class

grid_search = GridSearchCV(model, param_grid, cv=5)


# Fit the grid search to the data

grid_search.fit(X, y)
```

Chapter 20 - Random Walks

A random walk refers to a mathematical concept often visualized as a sequence of randomized steps across a defined mathematical space, such as the integers or the real line. These steps are influenced by a probability distribution. As a modeling tool, random walks are utilized to mimic various natural and societal phenomena, ranging from a molecule's trajectory within a gaseous medium to the fluctuating trends of stock market prices.

To summarize the main application fields:

- **Physics**: They depict particle movements, such as the diffusion of gas molecules or electron transitions in metals.
- **Finance**: In financial modeling, random walks shed light on stock market trends, foreign exchange rate fluctuations, and similar financial dynamics.
- **Computer Science**: Algorithms, including Google's PageRank, implement random walks to rank web pages based on significance.
- Beyond these, random walks find relevance in biology, epidemiology, image processing, and a myriad of other disciplines.

Random walks primarily fall into two categories: discrete-time and continuous-time. Discrete-time random walks operate in distinct time intervals – for instance, every minute or every hour. On the contrary, in continuous-time random walks, the progression occurs at arbitrary moments in time, dictated by a continuous-time stochastic function. For the scope of this article, the spotlight will be on discrete-time random walks.

Simulating Random Walks in Python

Python offers numerous methodologies to simulate random walks. A prevalent approach is employing the **random** module, an integral part of Python's core library. This module furnishes a slew of functionalities to spawn pseudo-random numbers, making it apt for simulating a random walk.

Suppose that we want to generate a random walk spanning 100 steps, leveraging the **random** module. We initialize the walk with a starting point of 0. We then generate 100 steps of the walk by flipping a coin at each step and moving one step to the left or one step to the right depending on the outcome of the coin flip.

```python
import random


# Initialize the walk

walk = [0]


# Generate the random steps

for i in range(100):

    step = walk[-1]

    coin = random.randint(0, 1)

    if coin == 0:

        step -= 1

    else:

        step += 1

    walk.append(step)
```

Alternatively, numpy's random package can also be used for generating random walk. With the code lines below, we will get the result.

```python
import numpy as np
```

```
np.random.seed(123)


steps = np.random.randint(0, 2, size=(100,))


walk = np.where(steps == 0, -1, 1)



walk = np.cumsum(walk)
```

Visualizing Random Walks with Matplotlib

Having generated a random walk, it's insightful to visualize its progression. For this purpose, the Matplotlib library in Python stands out. With its extensive plotting functionalities, Matplotlib facilitates the creation of a diverse range of graphics.

Let's see the code for generating a line plot of a random walk:

```
import matplotlib.pyplot as plt

# Plot the walk

plt.plot(walk)


# Add labels and a title

plt.xlabel('Steps')

plt.ylabel('Position')

plt.title('Random Walk')
```

```
# Show the plot

plt.show()
```

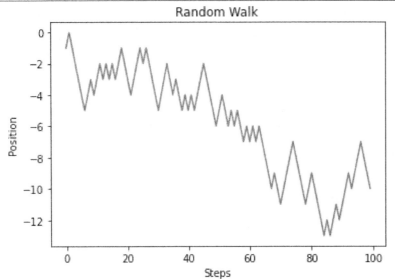

The code will yield a line graph showcasing the random walk (the x-axis identify the step count, while the y-axis displays the walk's position). Both axes will be labeled appropriately, and the graph will feature a descriptive title.

For those intrigued by two-dimensional random walks, Matplotlib provides the tools to visualize this as well. Here's how you can generate a scatter plot for a 2D random walk:

```
import matplotlib.pyplot as plt

# Generate the random walk

np.random.seed(123)


steps = np.random.normal(loc=0, scale=0.25, size=(100, 2))
```

```
walk = np.cumsum(steps, axis=0)


# Plot the walk

plt.scatter(walk[:,0], walk[:,1])


# Add labels and a title

plt.xlabel('X-Position')

plt.ylabel('Y-Position')

plt.title('2D Random Walk')


# Show the plot

plt.show()
```

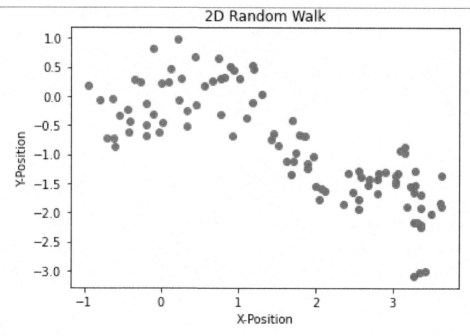

The resulting plot presents the 2D random walk, with the x and y-axes depicting the positions on their respective axes.

Analyzing Random Walk Patterns

The analysis of random walks can vary based on its application and the kind of data insights one seeks. Typically, researchers might delve into aspects like the average position, variability in steps, or the likelihood of the walk returning to its origin.

Here's how you can determine the average position of your random walk using the **mean** function from the NumPy library:

```
mean_position = np.mean(walk)

print(mean_position)
```

Output:

```
0.36761064525644427
```

Similarly, we can calculate the variance of the random walk using NumPy's **var** function:

```
variance = np.var(walk)

print(variance)
```

Output:

```
2.829563277966772
```

Now let's visualize the mean and the variance along with the random walks:

```
# Plot the walk

plt.scatter(walk[:,0], walk[:,1])
```

```
plt.plot(walk[:,0], [mean_position for i in range(len(walk))], c='m')

plt.plot(walk[:,0], [variance for i in range(len(walk))], c='r')
```

Output:

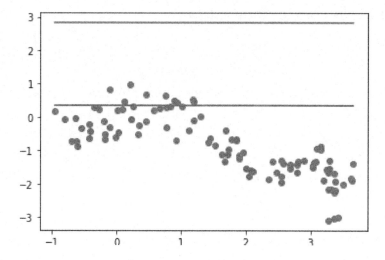

The red line shows the variance, and the purple line represents the average of the random walk.

Chapter 21 – Questions and Exercises

You can find the solutions (along with many other exercises and extra content) at the following web address:

>> http://www.readingroadspress.com/python-extra

1. How would you build a function that takes in 2 integers and computes their product, without using the * operator?

2. How would you build a function that takes in 2 integers and computes their quotient, without using the / or // operators?

3. How would you build a function that takes in 2 integers and returns the remainder of their division, without using the % operator?

4. How can you remove all duplicates from a list in Python while preserving the order of the elements?

5. How can I find the common elements between two lists in Python?

6. How can you convert a string of comma-separated values to a list of integers in Python? Take the string = '1, 2, 3, 4, 5' and convert it into a list of integer values.

7. How can you handle a specific exception (let's say ZeroDivisionError) and provide a custom error message?

8. How can you read a large file without loading the entire file into memory?

9. How can you write to a file in Python without overwriting its current content?

10. Let's say we have this list: My_list = [1, 2, 3, 4, 5, 6, 7, 8, 9, 10]. Using a for loop and indexing, how would you print every other element in the list?

11. Now, use a while loop to remove the occurrence of element 2 from my_list = [1, 2, 2, 3, 2, 4, 2, 5].

12. Let's say we have the following dictionary: my_dict = {'a': 1, 'b': 2, 'c': 3}. How would you use a for loop to create a new dictionary that contains the square of each value in the given dictionary?

13. How would you use scikit-learn's StandardScaler to normalize a dataset? Create a sample dataset using the np.array() method and use the StandardScaler to normalize the dataset.

14. How can you efficiently find the indices of the elements in a 2D numpy array that are greater than a certain value? Let's say we have this array: X = [[1, 2, 3], [4, 5, 6], [7, 8, 9]].

15. In this exercise, you are advised to create two 1D numpy arrays. Then find the intersection of the two arrays and return the indices of the matched elements in the first array.

16. Consider that you have this dataset: data = {'category': ['A', 'A', 'A', 'B', 'B', 'B'], 'sub-category': ['X', 'Y', 'Z', 'X', 'Y', 'Z'], 'value': [1, 2, 3, 4, 5, 6]}. You are advised to create a stacked bar chart that shows the percentage of each sub-category within a category, using matplotlib.

17. Using the Scipy module, find the global minimum of the following function: $f(x, y) = -(sin(x) + cos(y)) * exp(-(x^2 + y^2))$.

18. Build a deep learning model using Keras that can classify images of handwritten digits (from the MNIST dataset) with at least 99% accuracy.

19. Write a Python script that produces a random string of characters of a specified length, with the ability to include uppercase letters, lowercase letters, numbers, and special characters. The script should also validate that the string contains at least one of each of the specified character types.

20. Create a Python script that takes a list of integers as input and returns a new list containing only the prime numbers from the input list.

21. Write Python code that finds the second-largest number in a list of integers.

22. Let's say we have the following string: "This is a test sentence. This sentence is used to test the word count function." How can I find how many times each word is repeated in a given string using Python?

Extra Content

Uncover a treasure trove of extra content and additional resources waiting for you to explore and enjoy.

Scan the QR-code or follow the link below to access everything:

http://www.readingroadspress.com/python-extra

Printed in Great Britain
by Amazon

39060137R00110